40 Years of
Overcoming Cancer

40 Years of Overcoming Cancer

My Inspirational Story

JUSTIN COOPER

Story Terrace

Text Chris Hillman, on behalf of StoryTerrace

Design StoryTerrace

Copyright © Justin Cooper

First print October 2021

StoryTerrace

www.StoryTerrace.com

CONTENTS

PROLOGUE

When people learn that I lost my leg at the age of 17 from cancer, the first thing they always say is how horrific that must have been. From their perspective – from the outside looking in – I can completely understand why they would say that.

However, I can honestly say that, at the time, it did not feel 'horrific'. Before I had the limb amputated, I couldn't walk more than a few yards, my leg was agony every day. The chemotherapy they were giving me to prevent the tumour from getting bigger was not only failing to shrink the tumour but was also slowly killing me. So, in actual fact, the amputation saved my life, making it possible for me to get on with living. From the day my leg was removed, I felt that my whole life was ahead of me – and what a life it has been!

Yes, there have been dark days and times when I have cried and asked myself 'Why me?' But (as I have always told anyone who is dealing with illness or bad times) before you know it, those dark days are so far behind you it is hard to remember just how bad they were. It is true to say that the bad days do fade, especially when they are outweighed by good days. I have had so many good days – way more than I could ever begin to write about in this book.

I am convinced that, without the cancer, my life would have taken a completely different route; not only that, but I am positive that I would not have found half of the happiness in my life that I have now (even with only one leg). Admittedly, I was too young and naïve to fully understand the gravity of my situation when I was first diagnosed at 15 but, again, I am convinced that this helped me get through my diagnosis; as far as I knew, I had an illness, I went to the hospital to get treatment and got better ... end of the story.

My mantra has always been to try not to worry about anything until someone actually tells you something that you should be worrying about. For example, you have a test and you're waiting for the results. They could be good; they could be bad – why worry? If they're good, you've worried for nothing. If they're bad ... OK, *then* worry.

I think that, because of what happened to me in my teenage years, I have very much lived my life for today and have always made sure that I had something nice or fun to look forward to in the immediate future. I'm not saying that I never expected to live very long; I'm just saying I kept my life goals in the short term. However, I always have goals. At 53, I have already lived an amazing life and been to many wonderful countries, experiencing some exhilarating times. Modern medicine today is so far advanced from medical practice in the early 80s. In present times the treatment has improved so much that it, in itself, is not as invasive as it was, and hopefully, more and more people will go on to survive their own battle with cancer.

As I get older, I begin to hear more often of people I once knew, passing away from one disease or another and it always makes me realise just how lucky I have been.

If I died soon (and I'm not intending on dying soon!) I would have no regrets. I don't think there's anything that I ever wanted to do that I haven't done; my life has been my bucket list, and my wife, Lynn, is convinced that I am going to outlive everyone we know, including her!?

So, please try not to feel that your life is over if a doctor ever has to tell you that you have cancer. It's an episode that many of us may have to face at some time and to any degree, but it certainly doesn't have to mean it's the end. You must try to maintain a positive mindset and believe that, once you've had your treatment, you will get better, and your life will go on. I am living proof that this is entirely possible.

Justin Cooper

Lynn and I in our favourite city - Rome

1

THE FORMATIVE YEARS: THE BIGGEST DECISION OF MY SHORT LIFE

My story starts in the East End of London before my family moved to Essex. My dad was a builder, and in 1977 he built us a house in a quiet little village, Maylandsea, where I grew up. Like most kids, I had a group of friends to hang around with. My main passion was sport; we all loved to play football and ride our bikes, and I took up running. To be honest, I would give most things a go.

Those early days were quite normal: I went to school, played with my mates, and spent all my daylight hours kicking a football around the park. Academically, I must have been quite bright as I passed the '11 Plus', which meant I could go to grammar school. The nearest grammar school was in Chelmsford, a 45-minute bus ride away. Every weekday morning, I would wait for the bus to pick me up, while most of my friends would be jumping on a short bus ride in the opposite direction, as they all went to the nearby comprehensive school in Burnham-on-Crouch.

One day, Michael Robinson, a mate of mine who went to another school in Chelmsford but lived in our village, had a birthday party at our village hall and invited a number of friends from his school. Everyone's parents drove them there because they were only thirteen and they all lived in Chelmsford. One of the guests was a pretty girl, and I fell in love with her straight away.

As any young lad will know, at thirteen your hormones are running wild, and the opposite sex becomes very interesting all of a sudden. However, the object of my affection lived in Chelmsford, a whole 45 minutes away – obviously, I had no way of ever seeing her again. Not to be discouraged, I created a cunning plan with Michael, the birthday boy. He was in the same class as the girl, which gave us an idea; we agreed that Michael would lend me his spare school tie so that I could join my first love's class at school and see her every day. We managed to keep this up for a week, although the teachers did wonder who the new kid in class was, frequently asking 'Who are you, young man?' to which I would reply, 'I'm new, sir!'. After a few days, however, word got round that there was an imposter from the grammar school across town. A group of the bigger boys confronted me and chased me back out onto the street, jeering at me to go back to the 'posh school'.

Unfortunately, my plan was ruined. However, that was not the end of the story, as, by that point, my school had clocked my absence and had got in touch with my parents. They confronted me, saying that we'd all been summoned to the school for a 'chat'. This little chat resulted in me leaving the school and joining back up with all my mates at the comprehensive, which is where I wanted to be in the first place.

I was very sporty, as I have already mentioned, and especially keen on running – I would run three to four miles each morning before school. On one of these runs, I noticed a lump was developing on my left shin, just below my knee. As the weeks passed, the lump grew bigger and more painful. My mum took me to see Dr Warren, our local GP, who referred me for an x-ray. Initially, they told me there was a small fracture beneath the lump and that the lump itself was simply my bone calcifying over the injury. The solution was as simple as resting up for a while.

Unfortunately, the lump failed to get any better. At night, it would get hot and was extremely painful, keeping me awake. So, we went back to Doctor Warren, and it was clear he was frustrated with the original diagnosis. Bless him, he pushed for a full biopsy at the hospital. Again, we were told it was benign, and we all breathed a sigh of relief. Thank God, we thought, it was nothing serious. Regrettably, however, this relief was short-lived.

After several return visits to the doctor, he lost his temper with the hospital, as he was certain that there was something more serious going on. He tried to maintain his professional front, but he seemed prepared to put his job on the line to get to the bottom of my issue.

Finally, he got the hospital to agree to do a second biopsy.

This second biopsy was some ten months after the first, and by now the pain was unbearable. The process was similar to before; they opened the old wound, made the scar a bit longer and did what they needed to do. This time, we found that Dr Warren had been right, and his instincts were spot-on: the tumour was malignant. The doctor received the news on the day of my last school exam. Unaware of these developments, and as it was my first day of freedom, I set off on my bike with my mate Darren. We were heading to a girl's house, and I remember how excited I was about the summer ahead. When we knocked on the door, her mum answered it.

She looked straight at me, worriedly. 'You need to go straight back home,' she told me.

I turned round and cycled the five miles back home again. The hospital had been in touch with my parents. When I arrived home, my mum told me I'd been referred to St. Bart's in London.

Me, Darren, and our other mate Bryan were all fanatical about cars and motorbikes. We had all arranged to join what was then known as the Youth Training Scheme (YTS) as trainee mechanics for different local garages. Unfortunately, I was never to start that part of my life; instead, I would stay at Bart's for the foreseeable future

Back in the 1980s, as a teenager, I didn't know much about cancer. I actually thought it was entirely related to smoking, which was the big thing back then. I thought 'Oh no, mum and dad will know I've been smoking ... Now I'm in trouble!'

When we arrived at the hospital, the doctors couldn't decide whether I should be on an adult's or a children's ward, eventually settling on the former. My ward mates were much older than me, but we all got on great. This was the summer of 1984, and the Los Angeles Olympics were on. In those days, the ward would have just one TV, which sat at the end of the ward on a table with wheels. I would stay up all hours of the night while the 'old boys' were fast asleep.

As I was so young, the consultants were obviously very reluctant to amputate my leg as a first option, so they decided to put me on a course of chemo- and radiotherapy. The radiotherapy was done in a hyperbaric chamber. What was weird was that the treatment made my skin feel like plasticine; you could push your finger in and it would make a deep impression on the skin.

As anyone knows who has had the misfortune to need chemo, it does cause you to lose your hair. Sometimes it comes out in clumps, which makes you look awfully ill, so my mum shaved it all off for me. I looked like the actor Telly Savalas – 'Who loves ya, baby?' As well as hair loss, back then chemo drugs were less sophisticated and were well known for making you sick. I would go to the hospital, and the

15

nurses would stick a canular in my arm and pump me full of the drugs. In the words of Malvina Reynolds, there was a pink one, a red one, a blue one and a yellow one! A few hours after returning home I would start to feel sick, which would last for about a week.

Chemo kills fast-growing cells, which are what cancer is. The problem is, white and red blood cells are too – which, of course, means that your whole immune system deteriorates. I remember going in one time and the doctors decided I was too ill for chemo, so they kept me in on a ward until I was well enough to cope with it.

I guess I had two years between 1983 and 1985 that I spent going backwards and forwards to hospital. It became normal life.

After two years of chemo, amputation was raised as an option. I was able to play a part in that decision. The consultants told me that while the chemo was stopping the tumour from growing, it was not making it shrink or go away. I had reached a point where I didn't want to continue with chemotherapy, as it was literally killing me. The effect on my overall wellbeing, coupled with the state of my deteriorating leg, was so detrimental that I was awarded a blue disability badge (although back then they were orange).

I also became eligible for a Motability car, although I was perturbed to discover they were all light blue, three-wheeled and opening via a sliding door on the side. My dad had bought my mum a motor scooter, which I used to ride. I must have looked a sight, with my bald head and no meat on my bones, but it got me to clubs and parties with my mates.

I decided the amputation was the best option; after all, the treatment was killing me and I couldn't walk on my leg. A date was agreed. The day of the operation, I built myself up and we went to the hospital. When we arrived, there seemed to be various concerns about the procedure. Perhaps the surgeon had second thoughts, based on the fact I was only seventeen. I was told it wasn't going to happen and was sent straight back home again.

A few weeks later, I had a new date: 1st of May 1985. My driving test was booked for the 25th of May. My Mini Mayfair was all ready to go, and I would need a car more than ever after the amputation. So, we agreed to keep the test date and arranged for some lessons with the driving instructor beforehand. Our local driving instructor, who was also the treasurer of the darts team, was known as 'Steady' Eddie Hines. Everyone in the village passed their tests, thanks to Eddie.

The day of the amputation arrived, and I was full of nerves; my mind raced, wondering what to expect. I was about to lose a leg at the age of 17, yet once I had overcome the initial turmoil, I felt prepared for surgery; I'd come to terms with the idea that it was the only solution possible. All the pain, the discomfort, and the emotional rollercoaster I had gone through up until this point, were about to end. The leg I had grown to hate would soon be gone.

I recall waking up a few hours after the operation. Anyone who has been through amputation will know about the 'ghost pains' phenomenon. Ghost pains feel as though they come from the missing limb and can be excruciating. They can also manifest as maddening itches. When I woke up from the operation, I could still feel my leg. I wondered if the operation had even taken place. Slowly lifting the bedsheet, I saw my bandaged stump. My first feeling was shock, then fear, but I very quickly began to realise that this was going to be the start of the rest of my life.

A full head of ginger hair and my first Fred Perry

Shopping trip to Romford with my best mate Darren

My hair was just starting to grow back but I probably weighed about seven stone soaking wet!

2

'ST TRINIAN'S': NEW BEGINNINGS

The rest of my life started on the 1st of May, following the amputation of my diseased leg. Sitting in hospital, I suddenly had an ironic thought. 'I have had my leg amputated just above the knee in Hackney Hospital. Hack-Knee!'

I spent a couple of weeks recuperating in the hospital and started my rehab programme straight away. One of the methods they used involved connecting me up to an electronic pulse-type machine (much like those slimming pads you see advertised on TV). There were two small electrical pads that were fitted on either side of my stump (the vulgar name given to what remains of your amputated leg). A battery-powered electrical pulse was fed through the pads, the idea being that it would block the ghost pains that can happen following an amputation. You see, it takes a while for your brain to realise that the leg is no longer there; as such, you can still feel all the sensations you felt before it was removed: pains you cannot ease and itches you cannot scratch. The frustration still haunts me today.

During my stay in the hospital, I had various visits from my friends and cousins. During one of those visits, they asked me if I had been outside yet. I told them I didn't think I was allowed to yet, as I was only just getting the hang of using crutches in the ward and needed help getting around. At this point, remember, I still had the bandages on my stump!

'No worries,' they said, 'we'll find you a wheelchair and head to the pub over the road.'

'Hold up,' I said, 'it's only been a few days since I had my leg amputated!'

Undeterred, one of my cousins scampered off down the ward. After a little while, he reappeared, pushing a wheelchair. They all bundled me into the chair, with no permission or consent from any doctors or nurses, and we shot off out of the ward, into the lift and out onto the street. There I was, being wheeled along a busy Hackney Road dressed in pyjamas and a dressing gown, with my pulsing mechanism still attached and my heavily bandaged stump looking like a medieval battering ram.

Putting all our lives at risk, my cousins pushed me across the busy road and manoeuvred the wheelchair through the pub doors and up to the bar. I was convinced this was the local for the hospital doctors, as several people looked at me as if to say 'Should you really be in here? In your condition?' Nonetheless, we had a good old drink in the pub and a few laughs before my cousins returned me to the relative safety of the hospital ward.

As mentioned earlier, my driving test was booked for the 25th of May. I was determined to take it; I needed to, because I would never need a car more than I did now.

The driving centre where Steady Eddie would be taking me for my test was in Brentwood, Essex, and it was famous for just one thing; namely, all the driving examiners were men, apart from one lady. She had gained a fearsome reputation for being very tough and very strict – and no one wanted her for their test!

Eddie was giving me one last lesson before we made our way to the test centre. We parked up, then Eddie and I, with me on my crutches, walked into the waiting room and sat down, nervously listening for someone to call my name. Suddenly, an older lady with a clipboard and an angry-looking scowl appeared. She looked around the room and shouted out 'Justin Cooper?'

I looked at Eddie. He looked at me. I could subconsciously hear him saying 'Whoops, you're in big trouble now, son!'

I stood up, balancing myself on my crutches. Not giving me a second glance, she told me to follow her outside. Arriving in the car park, she asked me to read a number plate on a car a short distance away. Standard. Successfully read, we both got into my Mini Mayfair, her sitting primly in the passenger seat as I clambered my way into the driving seat.

Once I was in, she inquisitively looked me up and down over her glasses, evidently taking in my 'skinhead' haircut and missing left leg. 'Motorbike accident?' she enquired, abruptly.

I looked back at her, and confidently said 'No, I've had cancer.'

Her attitude changed in an instant. More enthusiastically, she asked me what hospital I was in. I told her it was St. Bart's and the ward I was on. She became even more animated – as it turned out, her niece was also in the same hospital, also receiving treatment for cancer. She was in the female ward, which was directly across from where I had been.

We got into a lively discussion about the hospital and the staff before I had to remind her about the driving test – which, of course, turned out to be an absolute breeze! Now, that could have been because I'm the greatest driver in history, but I'd like to think that she had a lovely warm heart in there really.

Driving test passed, and the Mini Mayfair purring away like a dream, I suddenly realised I was no longer confined to the tiny, remote village in which we lived. I was now free and could go anywhere I wanted. As Del Boy Trotter would say, the world was my lobster.

Being one of the first of my mates to pass their test, I automatically became the 'Friend Taxi'. I loved driving anywhere, taking mates to nightclubs such as Duke's in Chelmsford or Talk of the South (known as 'TOTS') in

Southend. Occasionally, we might have had six or seven of us in the Mini at a time! My mates would always make sure there was juice in the tank – I never had to put my hand in my pocket for petrol. They knew I wasn't well enough to work yet, so they always looked after me.

After a month had gone by since my amputation, it was time for my first visit to the limb-fitting centre at Hornchurch in Essex. The first thing you do there is get introduced to the physiotherapy team. The centre won't fit your new leg if you still have stitches in or if your stump is swollen. So, the physio team is there to help speed up the process, getting you ready to be fitted for a prosthetic. They start with a thing they called a pneumatic post-amputation mobility (PPAM) aid. This is similar to a swimming armband but is two feet long. They put one end over your stump before placing a metal leg-shaped cage over the bottom end. Next, they fill the PPAM aid with air. As it fills up, the sleeve grips both your stump and the metal cage, which has been measured to correspond with your leg length.

The physios then teach you, with the aid of crutches, to swing the PPAM aid in such a way that will encourage the muscles in your stump to work in the way you will need them to if you are to walk with your prosthetic leg. When your amputation is above the knee, the surgeons have to do a lot of work reshaping your muscles to protect the stump and to enable you to swing your new leg the right way. The physio to get you prepared for your prosthetic leg can take several weeks.

The next phase of the journey was to be introduced to the prosthetist, who is the person responsible for fitting and building your new limb. My prosthetist was a great guy called Roy Elliott. I liked Roy, as he was very friendly. He supported Fulham, so we talked a lot about football, and he seemed to have a lot of influence in the prosthetics department.

The first phase of having a prosthetic made was to have a plaster-of-Paris mould made of your stump, giving the prosthetist the exact shape and size of the socket needed. You didn't start with what is called a 'free knee'; instead, you started with the knee in the locked position and had to pull a lever on the side of the socket to bend it at the knee. Initially, it was safer to have a locked knee while you were walking and then, when you wanted to sit down, you unlocked the knee for it to bend.

I asked Roy when my leg would be ready to go. I told him I had a deadline of next Friday, as there was a party that all my friends were going to. Roy promised me he would do everything he could to have it ready for then. I knew he wouldn't let me down.

Friday arrived – I was so excited. I walked into the fitting room on my crutches and there it was: my brand-new leg, in all its glory. Admittedly, it wasn't the most attractive thing I had ever seen, made from a combination of rubber, leather and metal bits. It was very heavy, with levers sticking out, a big leather belt that went around the waist and another that went over the shoulder. However, when Roy got me into the leg, it fitted like a glove. He warned me to be careful, and with that, I goose-stepped out of the hospital and into my Mini for the drive home.

The party that night was at a favourite club of ours, called the Wick in St Lawrence. It was where all my mates would hang out. That night was billed as a 'St Trinian's fancy-dress party'. Looking for stuff to wear, I found an ancient school blazer that still fitted me, an old grammar-school tie and a cap from the cubs. Grabbing a pair of old school trousers, I cut them just above the knee, so that they looked like shorts.

I quickly got dressed up in my St Trinian's gear before standing in front of the full-length mirror in my bedroom. I have a great and vivid memory of the moment; for the first time in months, I was able to stand upright and unaided, with my shoulders the same height. I looked like a complete man – I almost felt 'normal' again. The thought choked me up a little.

I decided I wouldn't drive to the party as I wanted to have a drink, so my mum dropped me off. As soon as I walked in, someone noticed me and shouted, 'Justin's here!' Suddenly, I was overwhelmed with friends, some I hadn't seen since before the amputation. The girls were leaving lipstick kisses all over my chemo-bald head, the lads were hugging and squeezing me. It was utterly fantastic to feel normal and complete again, and to properly go out with my mates.

I didn't pay for a drink all night – they were such a great group of friends!

At seventeen we were doing a bit of drinking. We used to frequent a pub called the 'Virginian' (shortened to the 'Virgin'), which was run by two people called Rene and Kevin. Rene loved us: we were 'her boys'. We had our own table in the corner and personal tankards, later becoming part of the adults' pool and darts teams (with Steady Eddie, the driving instructor, being the treasurer for the latter).

We used to play both home and away matches all over the Dengie (the Dengie Peninsula, a region in Essex). I remember we were once playing an away match in Althorne, in a pub called the 'Sun and Anchor'. I remember because it was down to me to play the last singles game to see who won the overall match ... and I lost!

One of our team then thought it would be funny to throw a dart at my false leg, which was concealed by my trousers. It stuck in. The rest of the team thought this was hilarious, so they all decided to throw their darts at my leg. I played along with it and fell to the ground, screaming in agony and apologising for losing the match. The pub regulars were horrified at what they were seeing. This poor guy, being barbarically attacked with darts by his teammates for losing a pub darts match?

I couldn't hold it in any longer, I burst into laughter and started to take the darts out of my leg while explaining the story of my prosthetic limb to the horrified locals. That match and the look on the faces of the pub regulars that night will stay with me forever.

Another memorable night came in winter that year when I was driving around St Lawrence. I had a mate in the front seat and two female friends in the back. It had been snowing; I remember the roads were quiet so I was zigzagging to see if the car would slide a bit. Showing off, really. As we got nearer to the Wick, I came around a corner and in the middle of the road lay the large concrete base of a 'No Waiting' sign. There was no way that I could avoid it; as if in a slow-motion movie scene, the car went up in the air, flipped and rolled onto its roof.

The girls in the back were still screaming as the car came to a standstill. As they and my mate in the front seat unclipped their seatbelts, they all fell onto the roof of the upside-down car. When I did the same, however, I stayed exactly where I was – firmly attached to the driver's seat.

'This doesn't make sense,' I thought.

I then realised the foot of my false leg was trapped under the brake pedal. Realising the situation, I gave the leg a few sharp thumps before it released, and I came crashing down onto the roof of the upturned Mini with a thud. We then all crawled out and took refuge in the Wick.

Fortunately, that night no one was hurt. For my beloved Mini Mayfair, however, it was the final adventure. That night also became a milestone for me, as it was the end of my adolescence. Supposedly, anyway!

St. Trinian's - The first outing with my new leg. The lovely Dot on my lap – R.I.P.

Mid-chemotherapy here with my friend Simone

3

COMING OF AGE:
REACH FOR THE SKY

et's now move on to December 1985, my eighteenth birthday fast approaching. That birthday, my parents surprised me by telling me I was to have a party in the village hall. I later learned, in my early 20s, that they had been told I might not reach eighteen due to the seriousness of my condition, so maybe this was a celebration for them as well. The village hall was conveniently positioned next door to the 'General Lee' (the pub that Rene ran), which my mates and I had been drinking at for the last year. All my family and friends were at the party, and we were having a lovely time.

I heard a familiar voice call my name from behind me. When I turned around, there was Rene, standing in front of me holding a big present with a fancy bow on it.

Rene looked at me with an eyebrow raised. 'I am so delighted to be at your 18th birthday party, but it does beg the question; why have you been drinking in my pub for the last twelve months?'

It didn't matter – Rene loved us, 'her boys'. One of the ways that she showed her love for us was at Christmas time, when she would invite a few people around for a Christmas-night lock-in, we wouldn't have to pay for any food or drinks. Sadly, I learned a few years later that Rene had passed away and Kevin, who ran the pub with her, had moved to Ireland.

When you are eventually diagnosed with a primary tumour, the doctors need to establish whether any secondary cancers have appeared anywhere else in your body. For this reason, I was given a full-body scan, the results of which identified I had metastases in both of my lungs. The chemo had managed to shrink these tumours a little, but the doctors advised me that I would still require surgery to remove them. To do this, they have to go in through your back and break your ribs so they can access the lung that way. I ended up with a pair of ten-inch parallel scars on my back that look like curtains. The pain and discomfort of the procedure was so severe they would only do one at a time, so I had one done in May and then went off to America for a month to visit family. On my return, they took me in for the other side and I knew exactly what to expect. By now, the metastases were only the size of half a fingernail, so quite small. But they still had to come out.

The operation culminated in me needing a chest drain,

which is a tube that is stitched into your chest to release any build-up of blood in the chest cavity and lungs. On the day when the drain was to be removed, they began by giving me painkillers, which seemed a bit ominous. The reason for the painkillers soon became apparent. Once the chest drain had been removed, I had to stay in hospital until I could comfortably lift my arm above my head and was able to have a proper cough. It was a few days before I could do these things because the pain was so awful.

We've now reached the summer of 1986. By this point, I had received my cancer diagnosis, been pumped full of chemotherapy, had my left leg amputated above the knee and, finally, had both my lungs operated on to have the metastases removed.

Now it was time to look ahead to the future and get my first job.

Due to everything that had gone on in my relatively short life, I was already a good couple of years behind my mates, who had been in their YTS-scheme jobs for a while now. After looking around for a bit, I got a job in the county library headquarters in Chelmsford. If I'm honest, it wasn't my ideal job, but it was a job. My first job.

I found out that a friend in the village, Bridget, drove to Chelmsford every day, so we agreed to do a car share; I would drive one week, and she would drive the next. In those days I used to wear Kouros aftershave, because it was one of the most popular ones around. I loved it nearly as much as the ladies did – perhaps a little *too* much. I remember one morning I got up, splashed the Kouros all over, left the house and went to pick Bridget up. Immediately after she got in, she told me she found the Kouros atmosphere a 'little' overpowering. Hilariously, she had to spend the best part of the journey with her head hanging out the car window, gasping for fresh air. Needless to say, I tried to be just a little more conservative with the cologne from then on!

Although the job was boring, I made it my own and just got on with it. I think that, because it was my first job, it will always stick in my mind. However, I was feeling a little restless, and began to think about ways in which I could introduce some adventure into my life. I wanted to show everyone that, even though I had lost a leg, I was still a man: a 'butch and brave kinda guy'. One day, I saw an advert in the newspaper whose headline said, 'Jump for Cancer'. Upon reading the article, I found out that it was advertising the opportunity to do a parachute jump and raise money for cancer research at the same time.

'That sounds manly – and I've had cancer, so it's a cause that's now close to my heart. I'll apply!' I thought.

I got in touch with the organisers, and they soon contacted me with the disappointing news that I would not be allowed to do a static-line parachute jump, because the risks for an amputee were too great. However, they said I could do a tandem jump instead, which is where you are strapped to the front of an experienced instructor. I would go up to 10,000 feet and then freefall for a few seconds before opening the chute and drifting gently down to land. They noted that I wouldn't be able to do it with my leg on.

'That sounds exciting,' I thought, so the date was put in the diary.

The whole idea of the jump was to raise money for cancer research, so I needed to get some fundraising efforts underway. Rene put a sign up at the pub; *everyone* who came in was made aware of it and encouraged to sign up for sponsorship – Rene could be very persuasive when she wanted to be! We raised £1,650, which, back then, was quite a lot of money.

The big day came. The jump was to take place at Biggin Hill aerodrome, so me and my best mates, Darren and Bryan jumped into my car and headed for the airfield. As with all jumps, there was to be a briefing, it was surprisingly short. We got ready and I was introduced to my instructor, the man who would hold my life in his hands.

At the time, I guess I stood at around five feet ten tall. My instructor, who (mega-talented ex-Marine that he was) had done hundreds of jumps and was a wall of muscle ... stood at just over five feet tall. When we were tethered together, he was trying to talk to me about what to do, but his face was in the middle of my back, so all I could hear were muffled instructions coming from immediately behind me. The only bit I could understand was 'Hold onto the straps ... Don't hold onto the doors and, when we exit the plane, stretch your arms like wings. Look up and you will see the plane moving away'.

'Got it,' I thought.

Suddenly, from what seemed like nowhere, this tiny plane appeared; it had no doors and looked incredibly flimsy. I wasn't even sure it could get off the ground, let alone fly 10,000 feet in the air. We all climbed in, and it took off. I watched the needle move; 1,000, 2,000, 3,000 … all the way up to 10,000 feet, which my instructor confirmed by pointing to the dial of his altimeter. I got the nod and the thumbs-up sign, at which point we inched our way to the door, the wind rushing by the hole where the door should be and where we were about to take our leap of faith.

I recalled the instructions I was given: 'Don't hold onto the door, hold onto the straps.' Sitting on the edge of the doorway, I could feel the rush of the wind and then, suddenly, we were gone. I had an immense feeling of weightlessness, and my mind went blank for a second before I remembered to stretch my arms like wings. I looked up as I had been told to, but I couldn't see the plane.

The experience of plummeting towards the ground is incredible, although you don't actually feel like you're 'falling'. I was loving the feeling of the wind rushing against my face and the weightlessness, then I suddenly heard the guy shout, 'It's time to pull the chute!'

Now, like most of us, I always thought that when you pulled the chute you shot up into the sky, just like it looks on

TV. In reality, you just start to drift down more slowly; it's the speed at which the cameraman who's filming continues to fall that makes it look as though you shoot back up.

As the canopy opened, there was a moment of panic, and the joy of floating to the ground was interrupted by a tirade of muffled foul language from the middle of my back. As I tried to look around, I could see the instructor frantically pulling at the parachute lines. I looked up to see that the control lines were twisted, and so the chute had only partially opened.

My short 18-year-old life flashed before me as I thought 'I've beaten cancer, so I chose to jump out of a plane for charity. It's just my luck that I'm now about to die by crashing into the ground, slung beneath an out-of-control parachute!'

The muffled voice from the centre of my back said that we would have to spin to untangle the lines. By the time we stopped spinning, I was feeling dizzy and sick. I was, however, finally able to enjoy the remaining seconds of the jump before we made safe contact with the ground again, where Darren and Bryan were waiting to congratulate me. Boy, was I glad to be back on terra firma!

A little after we'd landed, the instructor congratulated me. 'Well done, son. I bet you didn't see the plane flying off, though, did you?'

'No, I didn't – why was that?' I asked.

It transpires that I had blacked out the moment we left the

plane; we were tumbling uncontrollably towards the ground for a couple of seconds before I regained consciousness and remembered to arch my arms ('like wings'), by which time, the plane had long gone. The whole experience was such a rollercoaster of emotions I would have struggled to drive home safely, so I asked Darren to take over the wheel. When we got back, we went straight to the pub, where everyone was waiting to hear how the jump had gone. Unsurprisingly, there were a few drinks drunk that night.

A short time after the jump, I received a letter from Cancer Research to say that the sponsorship I had raised was the second-highest amount raised by an individual that year, beaten only by a Metropolitan policeman. To acknowledge my achievement, they sent me two tickets to go to Lake Windermere for a presentation evening, so I took my mum with me.

The presentation evening was hosted by the diminutive Radio One DJ Bruno Brookes. That evening, I was acknowledged as the charity's second-biggest fundraiser; in recognition, Bruno and a holiday rep presented me with a free 18–30's weekend in Blackpool.

Amazing, hey? I nearly died, and so I got to go to Blackpool for the weekend!

I think it was early the next year when I started to have problems with my stump. The bone seemed to have become close to the bottom of my stump; as a result, it was becoming very sore. A trip to the doctors resulted in them suggesting that I may have had a growth spurt, and so the bone would need to be reduced by a couple more inches.

As I lay in my bed recuperating after the surgery, I had a pleasant surprise when four of the ladies from the library walked in. They had bought me the latest album by Luther Vandross (my favourite artist) and a pair of silk boxer shorts with hearts on. 'Classy,' I thought.

Surgery was becoming a way of life for me. The next phase of my rehab was to get re-fitted for a new socket, as my old one would no longer fit. It was another six weeks before I got to wear my prosthetic leg again.

I then began to think that, as lovely as my colleagues were, the library job was not for me. So, my friends started to ask around to see what might be out there; something more suited to my personality, perhaps. A friend worked for a local estate agent called Church & Hawes; I was told there was an opportunity to work with Terry, their mortgage advisor. If I got on with Terry, there could be a job for me.

In those days, once my hair had grown back, I was I real ginger nut. So was Terry. We were getting on well in the interview, laughing and joking and telling stories.

Suddenly, Terry went all serious, looked me in the eyes, and said 'Justin, can you make tea?'

'Of course, I can' I replied.

Through his very coarse, red beard he said, 'Good. We gingers need to stick together. There's a job here for you if you want it.'

That was the start of my journey as a trainee mortgage advisor and my first step into the field of finance.

I had also started a new relationship with Paula, one of the girls from the library. As you can imagine, I had a lot of personal insecurities, and I was especially uncomfortable in the presence of women. Paula was my first real relationship after having lost my leg, and I thought to myself 'Blimey, if I don't marry this girl, I might never find anyone else who will have me!'

Eventually, we decided that we wanted to buy a flat. It would cost us £50,000, and I wanted to put £5,000 down as a deposit. I used to give all my mortgage business to Mike, the manager of the local Abbey National. I went to see him and asked how much I needed to earn to get a mortgage of £45,000. I then went back to my boss at the estate agents and told them that I needed a letter to say I earned a certain amount of money (far more than I actually earned) in order to get the mortgage. They wrote the letter, and so Paula and I got our flat.

Paula and I got married and I was given my own Church & Hawes office to manage in Tiptree, Essex. One day, a flash car drew up outside my office, and a smartly dressed guy entered. He told me he was a head-hunter and asked me if I would like the opportunity to have a company car and an expense account like the reps that came and saw me. With no hesitation, I told him I'd love a job like that!

He introduced me to a man called Ken Petheridge, who worked for a company called MGM Assurance. The job came with a salary three times more than my current job paid, a company car and an expense account. I could get rid of my tired Morris Marina, swapping it for a brand-new Ford Escort.

Part of my induction at the company was a week-long residential training course in Worthing. On the final night, all the people on the course went out to a nightclub to celebrate. The club was upstairs, and I remember dancing the night away and enjoying perhaps a few too many drinks. It was then time to leave. We started to walk down the stairs and I missed the top step, stumbled, and fell all the way to the bottom of the stairs. I had cracked my head on the step as I went down, and sat dazed on the floor, rubbing the back of my head in pain.

The bouncer came rushing over, screaming to his mate to get an ambulance. I looked up at him to say there was really no need; after all, I had only banged my head and there was no blood.

I still remember the look of terror on his face as he shouted, 'It's not your head I'm worried about, it's your leg!'

He pointed over my left shoulder, and I turned to look. My leg had come out of its socket, twisted and was up behind my back, pointing in the opposite direction. You should have seen his face when I pulled it back into place, picked myself up and brushed myself down. I left him standing there with his jaw on the ground.

Another story for the archives.

Rene and Kevin who ran our local pub, The General Lee

4

GUESS WHO'S BACK:
DON'T BE AFRAID OF THE WATER

ooking back on my life, I realised that I had been ill for the formative years of my late teens and early twenties; those precious years when you go on holiday with your mates and discover just what the world has to offer. With that in mind, just before I got married, I took the opportunity to go on my first trip abroad with friends. Our adventure would take us to the glorious Spanish resort of Torrevieja.

This all came about because the man who owned the local video shop (our very own village Blockbuster) owned an apartment in Torrevieja and kindly offered it to us to rent for a week's holiday. This was perfect for our budget; all we had to do was find four cheap airline tickets and we would be on the Costa Blanca.

This was still back in the eighties, when music was our life blood and pop stars were icons such as Michael Jackson, Prince and Madonna. The favourite TV shows of the time were the A-Team, Airwolf and Miami Vice: Crockett and Tubbs were responsible for creating the fashion for pastel-coloured jackets with the sleeves rolled up, paired with linen trousers and espadrille canvas shoes.

We arrived in Torrevieja with sunglasses and espadrilles at the ready. The apartment was a little way out of the town, so we decided to walk in. The quickest way was along the beach – not an ideal surface for an artificial leg, but I was young, fit and up for it. The excitement of the bars and girls was enough to drive me on. We set off on the walk, with me dressed in a pair of shorts, a T-shirt, and espadrilles. I plodded along the sand with the boys until we got to the town. One of the lads then started to laugh, pointing down at my feet. It was only then that I realised that my espadrille had come off of my false foot, apparently about half a mile back. Obviously, I couldn't feel anything, so I was completely unaware of its loss. So now I'm in town with one shoe, much to the amusement of my friends – one of whom had seen it go and chose not to tell me!

Back home, I was always breaking parts of my false leg, due to being young and very active. Once, I purposely snapped off the lock on the knee, because the fashion was to wear very tight skinny jeans that would not pull up over the knee lock. Really, I had no other choice. These damages to the leg happened pretty frequently, which meant I was continually visiting the limb-fitting centre, so the staff and I got to know each other fairly well. As I was a pretty outgoing kind of character, they asked me if I would talk to other young amputees, to help them relax and feel better about the journey they were about to undertake. In return, I could just simply turn up and they would sort me out with whatever I needed, whenever I needed it.

One day, I was in the waiting room with other amputees and got talking to a young guy: a man-mountain, but with a false leg just like me. He'd lost his in a motorcycle accident when he was 19 but had managed to stay fit and worked out in the gym relentlessly. He asked me if I had heard of the British Disabled Water-Ski Association. I told him I hadn't. The guy said that the association catered for all sorts of disabilities and were based at a lake in Wrasbury, near Staines. As a young man who wanted to try as many new things as possible, this sounded right up my street, so I went down there one weekend to check it out.

At the lake, I was amazed at what I was seeing. I watched all sorts of people having a go at skiing: blind water-skiers going over a jump in the middle of the lake; paraplegic skiers in 'sit-skis'; and other amputees slaloming around the lake. It was fantastic to see people overcoming their disabilities in such an awe-inspiring way

Of course, I had to have a go. To begin with, I would start by holding onto a pole that jutted out from the side of the boat, which you used to help you get up onto your ski. I enjoyed the experience and managed quite well like this, so quickly moved onto the tow rope. With the rope, the technique was to let you float on the water, with the ski pointing up to the sky. Once you felt you had your balance, you would give the boat driver the command 'Hit it!'. As the boat accelerated across the water, you would roll up onto your ski; all you had to do was try and stay upright.

I loved it so much, I bought my own wetsuit. Obviously, being off the shelf, it had two legs, so I took it to a dive school and asked them to cut the left leg off. My suit was a 'steamer', meaning it let the water in and kept it in, allowing the heat of your body to warm it up. As such, the shortened left leg had to be sealed for it to work. The guys did a great job, and my personally designed suit was fit for purpose.

I had so much fun enjoying my new-found adrenalin rush that I went to the lake as many weekends as I could. During that summer, though, I developed a nagging cough, a cough I just could not get rid of. I first noticed it when I was skiing, but eventually it came on most of the time. It was driving me, and everyone around me, mad.

Eventually, I went to see my doctor, who took one look at my medical records and immediately saw that I had had two lung metastases removed about four years previously. Sensibly, he decided that the best thing to do was for me to go up to the hospital for an x-ray, which I did, the very next day.

I remember sitting at the table eating dinner the same night when the phone rang – around seven-thirty in the evening. When I answered it, it was my doctor, which seemed rather unusual; doctors don't normally call at that time of night. The doctor was quite forthright in telling me that the x-rays showed that I appeared to have shadows on both my lungs. He continued to say that he had arranged an appointment for me at St Bart's the very next morning, and so I needed to pick up the x-ray films (as they were back then) so that I could take them with me to the appointment.

This was a whole new ball game compared to when I was a naive 15-year-old that didn't understand what was going on. Now I was 24 and could adapt to new circumstances much more intelligently. I understood the gravity of the situation I was presented with.

When I put the phone down, the reality of what the doctor had just told me engulfed me. I was in shock; I thought that this could be the beginning of the end. It is difficult now to try and put into words exactly how I felt that night, but 'frightened' wouldn't really do it justice. I was absolutely terrified, and I must have asked myself 'Why me?' a hundred times. I cried. I couldn't understand why this was happening to me, and this time I wasn't so sure I could beat this thing.

I went to the local hospital that night and collected the large brown manilla envelope that the x-rays were put in back then. When I got home, I called my mate Mark, who came over straight away. Mark was very supportive, and he did his best to try and help lift my spirits. The football was playing on the TV, meaning that the screen was mainly all green (for obvious reasons) so Mark had an ingenious idea. We would slice open the manila envelope and put the x-rays up against the TV screen; the bright green background would then allow us to closely examine the contents of the translucent photographs of my chest.

There were two x-rays inside: one for each of my lungs. Although not a doctor myself, I could clearly see a round blur at the bottom of my left lung, but, to my untrained eye, there appeared to be nothing unusual on my right. I didn't really have a clue what I was looking at, but strangely I had a small amount of comfort in the 'knowledge' that my situation might not actually be as bad as I had first thought. We carefully resealed the envelope, ready for the appointment the next day, at which point I had a couple of stiff drinks to help me sleep and took myself off to bed.

We arrived at St Bart's and waited for my appointment with the thoracic surgeon. Once inside his consult room, he took out the films and proceeded to hang them up on the large light box that hung on the wall. I, of course, already knew what he was about to see.

After a few moments he turned and explained to me confidently, 'I can clearly see that there is a tumour in the lower lobe of your left lung, but nothing untoward appears in your right'.

I was amazed to hear that my totally non-professional self-diagnosis was right. I felt a little pleased with myself; all those hours of watching *Casualty* had finally paid off!

The surgeon said that the good news was that the tumour was entirely in the lower lobe of the left lung; his plan, therefore, was to remove the whole of the lower lobe, which would mean that the whole of the tumour would be gone, with no need for any more chemotherapy. The remainder of the left lung would simply expand into the space created in the chest cavity and, hopefully, I would barely notice any difference in my breathing.

My only concern then was that they would have to go through my back as they had done previously; I knew exactly just how painful that was going to be, as it had probably been the most painful of all the procedures I had been through up until then.

When the day came, they went through the existing left-hand scar on my back, removed the lobe and stitched me back up. I was going to need a few days in hospital and to have the dreaded drain placed in my chest, as before. Again, I needed to be able to comfortably raise my arm above my head and cough easily before I was allowed home. And, again, we all hoped that this was going to be the end of this particular cancer journey, and that perhaps I could now get on with my life.

This was around 1994 and, due to the journey I had made, I had become a mature young man who was able to deal with the reality of certain situations with a much wiser head than perhaps my years would have suggested. I knew that many things in my life were just not right, and that they had to change.

As mentioned earlier; I married Paula at the age of 20 which, for anyone really, is young. For me, it was because I was very insecure at the time, and I just didn't think I would ever find anyone else to love me again; therefore, I felt I had to get married to make sure that I wasn't going to be alone for the rest of my life.

Now, I know (as an adult) how silly that sounds, but when I was 20, with one leg (and ginger hair!) that's exactly how I felt.

Deep down, even though we both tried to make it work, we were very different people, leading very different lives. Eventually, we both realised that the relationship could not continue. So, after about five years of marriage, we agreed to separate. I was around at a friend's house playing computer games one night and, when I arrived home, Paula's dad had been, collected all her stuff and she was gone. That was that.

I woke the next morning, sad that we had not been able to make it work but, on the other hand, relaxed in the realisation that this was the next phase of my journey. At nearly 26, I was a single man again, and I had the rest of my life in front of me. I was determined to grab life with both hands and enjoy every moment along the way.

I was always a massive West Ham fan; however, I had not been to a game for years. So, one of the first things I did was to look at the fixture list. They had a home game the very next Saturday. I bought a ticket, went on my own and loved everything about it. The crowds, the sausage and chips, buying a programme – even the football! After the match, I immediately made the decision that I would go again next week. I scanned the fixture list again and saw that they were playing away, against Aston Villa. Although I had a car, I had never been to Villa Park before, so didn't fancy driving on my own. I found out that the club put on supporter coaches, so I decided to buy a ticket and go by coach.

I was on my own again, so I sat in the second row next to a guy whose mate was clearly sat in the seat just in front of us; they were chatting to each other around the side of their seats. I asked the guy if he would like to sit next to his mate and I would move into the front seat, next to another stranger. Decision made, I swapped into the seat in front and plonked myself down next to this grumpy-looking fella.

Me and the fella got talking (he wasn't really grumpy, as it turned out) and I found out that his name was John Carey. We went to the Villa game together, laughed and joked about our West Ham experience and found we had a lot in common (West Ham, mainly). We went on to follow West Ham together all over the country and toured the world following England. I ended up being godfather to his youngest daughter, and he eventually was my best man. We still go to football together to this day.

Now, over the years, John and I have had many adventures; some good, some not so good. I remember one occasion when West Ham played away against Liverpool. We couldn't get tickets in with the Hammers fans, but we knew somebody (who knew somebody) who got us two tickets in the 'Kop end', sitting with all the hardcore Scouse fans. Due to traffic, we arrived five minutes late, and West Ham were 1–0 down already. By halftime, they were 4–0 down. We decided this was no fun whatsoever and left to start the long drive home. We listened to the commentary on the radio in the car only to hear it was five nil thanks to ex–West Ham player Paul Ince. We had made the right decision to leave when we did!

It was a long way to go for forty minutes of football, but that's what we used to do for fun.

15/06/2006

John and I following England during the World Cup in Germany. Bumped into Marlon Harewood!

5

CATCHING UP WITH OLD FRIENDS: THE GOOD AND BAD

So, it was 1994 and I was about to enter the next phase of my life. I had become a single guy again, but I was living in the marital home on my own and so took in a few mates as lodgers. It would help with the mortgage, be a bit of fun and give me some company.

I read somewhere that the most stressful things you do in life are:

- Getting married
- Getting divorced
- Moving house
- Starting a new job

Unbeknownst to me, I was about to embark on three of them (all four of them, eventually). I was working alone in the office one day, when the phone rang. It was Steve Painter, the head-hunter, again. He asked me if I would be interested in another new job, this one with Allied Dunbar, which paid even more money and offered an even better car. Now, I knew Allied Dunbar was known for giving its guy's BMWs – I had always fancied a 'Beemer', so my answer was immediately yes.

Steve arranged for me to meet the local manager; a lovely lady called Jo Ranger. Jo and I got on really well straight away, and I knew almost immediately that I would be happy to have her as my boss. From her side, she could see that I had loads of enthusiasm and a great will to succeed, so she was eager to get me on board.

I asked her what the next steps were. With large companies such as Allied Dunbar, the employee medical cover was an important part of the package. Obviously, I had to be totally honest with her and tell her about my amputation, the removal of the metastases and the tumour that had come back five or six years later. I was really concerned that this could be a sticking point in my application.

Jo arranged my second interview, which was to be with the area sales director, a nice guy who explained that he would like me to have a medical with the company doctor. He went on to say that he would not be comfortable to have me on board without the same medical benefits as everyone else. I realised now that my medical could potentially determine whether I had a future with Allied Dunbar or not.

I had the medical, and the report came back a few days later. I nervously awaited the news. Later that week, the area sales director called me to explain that, although I was a higher risk than most, I actually only represented a small risk to the overall company, which had over 2,500 employees. They had decided that they wanted me enough to take that risk and the job was mine if I wanted it. Of course, I grabbed it with both hands.

At the time of getting the job, I was living in Essex and the job itself was in Watford, Hertfordshire. I convinced the company that the daily commute around the M25 would not be a problem, so they were happy to let me do that every day as long as I wanted to.

Initially I didn't get the BMW – I think my first car there was a brand-new Honda Prelude. Being in my twenties, as it is with most young men, the car I drove was very important; it represented what I had achieved in life. I would proudly sit behind the wheel with my shades on feeling a million dollars.

I commuted every day, and I have to say it was hard going; after about six months of sitting on the M25 every morning and night I had gotten sick of it. I was working with a great bunch of guys; one day we were talking and a couple of them said they house-shared near the office. They said they had a lady living with them who was leaving to move to Scotland, meaning that there was a room available. If I was interested, they'd be happy for me to move in.

I had a word with my cousin, who was lodging with me at the time, and told him I was thinking of moving and suggested he could buy the house from me. That's exactly what he did. It cleared the mortgage and didn't leave a lot left over, but I just thought 'sod it' – I wasn't worried about that, I just wanted to live my best life.

Literally a couple of weeks later, I moved in with Rob and Pete. Now, this house resembled the house in the *Young Ones* with Adrian Edmondson and Rick Mayell. A host of different women would come and go every weekend (none with me, I hasten to add) and we would argue about cleaning the toilet, food, who was responsible for what on the phone bill – just about everything, really. It definitely was a bachelor pad, and we were just like the characters in the TV series. At the same time, though, we had a lot of fun; we worked hard and played hard and had a great laugh.

I was sitting working in the office one day and a couple of other guys came up to me. One of them asked me what I was doing for my summer holidays. I thought to myself, 'Hang on a minute – I'm single. I can do what I want!'.

I told him I didn't have any plans.

'Why don't you come away with us,' he said. 'It'll cost you £350 for a week in glorious Lanzarote.

The decision took only a heartbeat. 'I'm in,' I said.

By the time the departure day came, I'd been single for about six months. We arrived at the airport, picked up our rental car, threw the suitcases in and headed off in search of our apartments in full anticipation of an amazing week in sunny Lanzarote. It was the summer of 1994; I remember this vividly because the World Cup was in the USA and

England had not qualified. Like any lads' holiday (and especially one in a World Cup year) we all wore football shirts; the other lads were Swindon Town supporters, which was a bit embarrassing but their problem, not mine. I wore the claret and blue of West Ham with great pride.

So, we arrived at our apartments, threw our cases into the rooms and headed straight down to the pool. We noticed a group of good-looking girls and decided to quickly get acquainted. It turned out they all worked in the cosmetics department of Rackham's, the department store in Birmingham.

At this point I guess it was still fair to say that, with everything that had gone on before; my confidence was a little bit shaky. That said, the girls and us seemed to gel and we all got on well. One day, me and the three lads decided we would do a little tour of the island, so hired an open-topped Suzuki Vitara Jeep. We all jumped in and off we went, with me sitting high up on the back seat, hanging onto the roll bars for dear life. The sun was blazing, the wind was in our faces; this was to be a day of real adventure. We were having far too much fun to worry about silly things like sun protection, not until later that evening. Me being a real redhead meant I was in big trouble; my back had been fried in the red-hot sun. It was on fire, and I had developed blisters as big as fried eggs.

As I mentioned earlier, the girls from our apartments worked in the cosmetics department at Rackham's, so if anyone would know about skin protection it would be them. Anyway, we were all sitting around having a drink before heading out for dinner and I was moaning about being burnt. Sarah, one of the Rackham's girls, said she would rub some aloe vera into my back to try and ease the pain and help the blisters heal. That was the start of Sarah and I getting to know each other.

It's amazing how quickly a week in the sun in the company of a great bunch of guys and girls disappears. It was soon time to put the football shirts and swimming shorts back in the cases and head for the airport. Time for us all to return to the reality of our home lives back in the UK. On our return, Sarah and I continued to stay in touch. 'Home', for Sarah, was in Walsall in the West Midlands, while I was still in Hertfordshire. We agreed that when Sarah finished work on a Saturday afternoon, she would come down to mine and stay until Monday night, before returning home, ready for work again on the Tuesday. This seemed to be a good compromise and kept our long-distance relationship going.

Way back before you could rely on the internet for everything, sports information (including details of football matches and what your club was up to) was all on a thing on the TV called Ceefax. One day, I was looking on the West Ham pages when I saw that they were to play a testimonial match, away to Exeter City, for a player called Eamonn Dolan. This caught my eye because I went to school with

Eamonn and his twin brother Patrick; they were fantastic all-round sportsmen and excellent footballers in particular. Our school team never lost a game with the Dolan brothers in it.

The Ceefax message continued to say that Exeter City would play at home to West Ham United the following night at 7.30pm. I thought to myself, 'I've got to go, it's an evening kick-off. I could easily leave work early and get there on time.'

So, I phoned John to tell him all about it and we agreed to set off for Exeter after work the following day. The next day comes and I was sitting in the office all excited about the game. Then I thought, 'I wonder if I could get to meet up with Eamonn?' But how would I go about doing that? I had left that school in the third year, which was about thirteen years ago; we never stayed in touch, so would he remember me? If so, how could I set it up?

I got on the internet and looked up Exeter City football club, finding its phone number.

I rang and spoke to a lovely lady, saying 'This is a long shot, but I know there's a testimonial on tonight for Eamonn Dolan and I will be coming along. I used to go to school with him and wondered if there was a chance, I could possibly get a message to him?'

The lady replied, 'He's not here at the moment, but would you like his home phone number?'

Amazing – she actually gave me his home phone number.

Can you imagine that today? 'Er hello, I went to school with Lionel Messi, could I please have his home phone number?'

Anyway, I hesitantly phoned Eamonn's home number. A lady answered, it was his wife. I apologetically told her that the club had given me his home number. I explained that I went to school with him and that I was going to the game that night and asked whether there was a chance of meeting up with him. She said he wasn't in at the moment, but that it sounded like a lovely idea. I passed her my mobile number so that he could call me back.

As planned, John and I jumped into the Prelude and headed to Exeter. As we were approaching the ground, the phone rang. It was a mobile number I didn't recognise. I picked it up and it was Eamonn, who said he'd meet me at the ticket office. Sure enough, when we arrived, Eamonn was there waiting for us. He hadn't really changed a bit! It turned out he was having a testimonial because he had recently had testicular cancer, which had cut his playing career short. When I discovered this, I immediately felt a sense of empathy with Eamonn because I knew what he must have been through. He had moved into management and was to become the Exeter City manager.

Patrick, his twin brother, had flown over from Ireland, so it was a brilliant little reunion. We all sat just behind the dugout and watched the game. After the match, Eamonn had arranged for us to meet up in the players' lounge, where we could enjoy a drink together, along with the entire West Ham team. What an experience that was! I met all the players and Harry Redknapp, the manager. I am still in touch with some of the old West Ham players I met that night. It was certainly an occasion that will live in my memories for a long time.

Sadly, Eamonn's cancer came back in 2016, when it finally took his life. Not, however, before he had moved across the country to be the youth team coach at Reading. He later became interim manager (when Brian McDermott was sacked) and made a cameo appearance on *Match of the Day*, when Reading played Manchester United. It was so wonderful to see my old schoolmate on TV. After he had passed away, I strangely felt very proud; he was so well respected at Reading FC that they named a stand in his honour at the Madejski Stadium: The Eamonn Dolan Stand.

It was sad to see someone I knew, who was so young and so talented, lose his life to cancer. Unfortunately, cancer is responsible for taking the lives of so many young people prematurely.

My life continued; I carried on working and keeping up my long-distance relationship with Sarah. I was up at the limb-fitting centre one day when Roy asked me if I would talk to a young man who had lost his leg in a car accident. I spent about an hour with the lad; quite understandably, he was still getting to grips with losing a limb, but I hoped that my chat gave him some comfort about his future on a prosthetic leg. After the conversation, I mentioned to

Roy that I had been getting some shooting pains down my right leg. Roy looked puzzled and said that I should see the doctor. There was always a doctor at the centre who was on hand for the medical side of things.

Roy took me up the corridor to the doctor's office and asked if he would examine me for the pains I had been getting. After a bit of poking and prodding, the doctor said that he would like to send me for a biopsy on my pelvis, as he had found some swelling there. The doctor referred me to the Royal National Orthopaedic Hospital in Stanmore Middlesex. I went in for the biopsy, which was done under general anaesthetic. They put you to sleep and then, using something that resembles an apple corer, they take a sample of your pelvis in four locations: top and bottom, on the front and back of your pelvis.

About a week later, I returned to get the results. I met with the doctor who had carried out the biopsies, and he broke the news to me at once.

'Justin, there are signs of a tumour in your pelvis.'

My heart sank. This was now about five years since the lung situation; I remember placing my hands over my face to try and prevent the doctor from seeing the fear that had just hit me. 'Why me?' I thought. 'Haven't I been through enough already?'

I felt the fear again but this time it was different, as I was alone. Yes, Sarah and I were in a long-distance relationship, but we saw each other for two days at a time every other weekend. How would I introduce this catastrophe into our three-month-old relationship?

That was a conversation that I couldn't think about right now. My immediate thoughts drifted to what treatment they might have in store for me this time. I was told I would need to become a patient of the hospital and would be under the care of Professor Tim Briggs, who was a specialist in bone tumours. Mr Briggs and I would eventually go on to have some life-changing decisions to make.

But first, back to St Bart's for more chemotherapy!

Me and the Dolan twins, Patrick and Eamonn, who sadly passed away due to Cancer

6

HAVE FAITH:
A MOMENTOUS DAY

Returning to St Bart's for some more chemotherapy was kinda depressing, as I distinctly remember the last time and how it made me feel incredibly sick and weak. Having chemo is mostly a very unpleasant and exhausting experience.

I was told by the clinicians they were going to put me on a new regime, one that lasted for seventy-two hours. This would take place over the course of a weekend; I would arrive on a Friday night and leave on the Sunday. I asked what this new programme consisted of, and they said they would pump my body full of saline solution for eight hours, before administering the initial dosage of chemotherapy. They would then flush my body with another eight hours of saline before giving me the anti-sickness solution, and then another eight hours of saline to finish that session. This would be repeated from Friday to Sunday.

I was curious to understand why so much saline needed

to be pumped through me; after all, all I was going to do was pee it out every few hours. The answer they gave made complete sense: it was important to keep the drugs and chemicals that would be pushed through my body in such a short space of time flushed from my kidneys, primarily to prevent the drugs from causing any unnecessary damage.

This process was a new approach to the chemo that I had received back in 1983. Back then they would put a cannula in my arm, pump me full of drugs and send me home, where, after a short while, I would be violently sick. That would take a few days to pass and then, once I stopped feeling sick, the whole process would begin all over again. How different this new approach was, and the reasoning behind it, would only really gain any significance to me later.

In any case, come Sunday night I would feel fine; fine enough to want to drive to the nearest McDonalds and get a couple of burgers down me, as, surprisingly, I was starving. This was not the chemotherapy I remembered from 1983.

The one common element to my earlier chemo treatment was that, after a short while, my hair would start to fall out, leaving me with little tufts of hair. So, I did what I did the first time around and shaved it all off. It is often hard to understand, but when having chemo, you literally stop growing hair *everywhere*. The chemotherapy kills the hair follicles, so it just doesn't grow. I even didn't have to shave anymore. I also started to lose weight; my appetite was up and down, but mainly down after the initial post-hospital desire for food. I just couldn't keep anything down or, more importantly, face-eating or even smelling food.

I do remember one evening, though; me and the boys were in the house when I suddenly got a craving for a single McDonalds cheeseburger (no pickles – I wasn't that sick!). I told them, after several days of barely eating a single morsel, that the one thing I fancied now, more than anything, could be got from the Golden Arches. Rob, bless him, jumped up, got in his car, and set off for the nearest McDonalds, a good fifteen minutes' drive away. He brought me back the burger and it came as a meal deal with a drink and fries. I didn't care for the ancillary items; it was just the burger I craved. It didn't take long to demolish; in fact, it barely touched the sides. When I jokingly said to the boys, 'I could easily eat another one of those!', Rob jumped straight up, got back into his car and repeated the journey for the second time in twenty minutes. That's what friends are for.

During this second bout of treatment, I lost a lot of weight; so much so that my stump had reduced in size, meaning I could no longer wear my false leg and spent my time permanently on crutches.

All through this period, Sarah and I had continued our long-distance relationship. On one of her visits, we sat down and talked about our future together. For me, as much as it was lovely to see Sarah on a regular basis, I didn't think it was fair on her to keep travelling down all this way when all she could do with our time together was not much more than nurse me. However, she disagreed, and told me that she was going to pack up her job, leave the comfort of living in her parents' home, look for a new job near where I lived and move down to live with me in the 'Young Ones' house. All that, just so that I didn't have to deal with this on my own.

True to her word, she found a job, moved in and started to care for me; she drove me to the hospital and was there when I had my treatments. Throughout everything, she was incredibly supportive.

It wasn't long after Sarah had moved in that my best mate Darren told me he was going to marry his long-time girlfriend, Jane. Although not feeling great and unable to wear my leg, I was determined not to miss his stag do – or, indeed, their wedding.

Darren's stag do was held in the local Chinese restaurant near to where he lived, called the Rickshaw. I knew the restaurant well (because, of course, I used to live near there too). I remember the evening vividly, mainly because I didn't have much of an appetite and was sitting next to a couple of mates and a great big plate of noodles! To give you an idea about the sense of humour we had with regards to my situation, one of them thought it would be hilarious to scoop up a big handful of noodles and plonk them on my head, like noodle hair. It was funny, and certainly drew a few strange looks from the other diners.

Darren's wedding was a week later; Sarah and I drove over to be there. I remember lasting through the ceremony and part of the evening before driving home, completely exhausted.

My health was not great during this period. At one point, in 1995, I was lying in bed watching the Everton vs Manchester United FA Cup Final. I remember one minute watching the game, then the next having a 'funny turn', needing an ambulance and ending up in hospital with some kind of infection. These were tough times, and the places you go when you're embroiled in the darkness of chemotherapy are nowhere nice. At times, it's difficult to see better days ahead. But I promise you, they do come.

During this latest run of chemo, a friend of mine from work, who knew I was a big West Ham fan, had a client who was a good friend of Harry Redknapp. Well, one day when I was sat up in bed and a nurse approached with her hand stretched out and an envelope in it. Rarely would you receive cards by post in hospital, they normally came with the visitors! Straight away, I noticed the West Ham United badge on the front of the letter.

Immediately, I was very curious as to what was inside. When I opened the letter, it turned out to be from Harry Redknapp, saying that he had heard I was a big West Ham supporter but was struggling at the moment with my health. Harry's message went on to say that, when I was well enough to get in touch with his secretary, she would arrange for me to meet the players and him at the training ground in Chadwell Heath.

When I got out of hospital, I contacted Harry's secretary and arranged to go to the training ground. The day of my visit, West Ham were playing a game against Arsenal. Harry asked me if I had tickets, and I took pleasure in telling him that I was a season-ticket holder.

'Tonight, don't go straight to your seat,' Harry said. 'Come to the directors' entrance and ask for me.'

My long-time football buddy John drove us to the stadium, and we parked in our usual spot. As we started to do our normal walk to the stand, I simply said to John, 'Let's go this way for a change.'

As we got to the directors' entrance, I went across to the guy on the door and told him, 'Harry Redknapp is expecting me.' The look of astonishment on John's face was a picture!

The doorman came back and told us to follow him, which we did – straight into the West Ham changing room. So, there we were, in the dressing room talking to players just before the match against Arsenal. It was all a little surreal. And the experience didn't end there; Harry told us, at the end of the game, to wave a steward down and get them to bring us to the player's lounge for a drink. All in all, that was one fantastic evening for a couple of devoted West Ham fans!

Shortly after this time, I finished my round of chemotherapy and was due to meet Mr Briggs at the Royal National Orthopaedic Hospital to discuss my hip. At the appointment, Mr Briggs told me to come in Sunday evening and expect to have surgery on the Monday.

I arrived with my mum, Sarah and one of Sarah's friends. As I remember, the ward was virtually empty. At around seven in the evening, Mr Briggs turned up and pulled the curtain around the bed.

He gave me that steely consultant look. 'Since I first met you in my clinic, I have not stopped thinking about you and what to do about your pelvic tumour. The surgery I had planned for you tomorrow would change your life forever, as I would have to remove the right half of your pelvis. However, this would mean that you lose your right leg and spend the rest of your life in a wheelchair.

'I can't even guarantee that this operation will cure your cancer. What's concerning me is that, right now, you have some quality of life – you work, drive, live in a house and can get around. Having this operation tomorrow would change all that.'

He paused. 'So, I have decided to send you home tonight, and I am going to have another think about what we can do and then get back to you.'

For the second time in my life, I had gone to the hospital expecting major surgery the next day and then been sent home. What an emotional rollercoaster! On the one hand, I was relieved not to be having half my pelvis removed, but, on the other, confused as to what the future had in store for me.

That night, my mum and I were talking, and she

mentioned my brother Perrin. Perrin was very different to me; he was a big believer in the spiritual world and had been to many spiritual fairs. He had mentioned a faith healer called Oliver to my mum; Oliver lived in Westcliff-on-Sea and had a reputation for doing some amazing things. I was a big sceptic, as I put my belief in science and the clever people who spend a lifetime trying to understand it. That said, everyone around me – including Sarah – said we should try every avenue. So, for them really, rather than for me, I agreed to meet with Oliver.

Sarah and I made the journey down to Westcliff to see this guy one Saturday afternoon. Oliver was a rather strange-looking chap, he had clearly been through some sort of trauma earlier in his life and this had resulted in a kind of misconfiguration of his head. As the story goes, when he was much younger, he was involved in a serious car accident – an accident he should have died in. But, in Oliver's words, he was visited by spirits who told him that he had a higher calling in life, and that he had been placed on this earth to heal people. For that reason, as he tells it, he survived.

Oliver was an incredibly humble person; he lived with his elderly mother and didn't ask for any money for doing what he did. He said that, if I wanted to pay something, I should simply donate to my favourite charity.

I sat in a chair, and Oliver asked if he could put his hands on my body. He explained his methodology, saying that it was a very 'hands on' approach. As he placed his hands on me, I could feel an intense heat. At this point, he had not asked me, and I had not told him, what the problem was. He slowly moved his hands over my body; as he approached my hip, he stopped, and said he could feel immense energy around that area. He asked if this was the area of concern, to which I said yes.

Before we left, he gave me a crystal and told me to rub it at night. We then left, with me still feeling very sceptical about the whole experience.

The following week, I had another appointment with Mr Briggs so that he could update me on his latest thoughts regarding how he planned to treat the tumour in my pelvis. At this meeting, he first reiterated his concerns that the surgery he had planned would not save my life. However, he was working in conjunction with an oncologist called Dr Anna Cassoni at Middlesex Hospital. Dr Cassoni was pioneering a new treatment, and they thought that I might be the perfect patient to trial it.

It was all very experimental; still based on a concept, even. However, Mr Briggs said that, if I was prepared to take part, it could do me some good. The least they could hope for was to make surgery a more viable option.

Mr Briggs explained that I would go into hospital and be given an injection of radium. They knew they could give radium in larger doses to terminally ill patients, because it would go straight to the bone tumour. At the time, radium was being given as a form of pain management, but only to terminally ill patients. The plan was that I would go into hospital and be given a small dose of radium, followed by six weeks of radiotherapy directed specifically at the point where the tumour was.

I went into hospital and had the isotope injection, and then I was put into what looked like a padded cell. It was a lead-lined room with slits in the door so food could be passed through. The arrangement is referred to as 'barrier nursing'. I lived like this for three days and then, on the third day, a man entered looking like something out of a sci-fi movie wearing a hazmat suit, who screened me for radiation with a Geiger counter.

I was given radiotherapy every day for six weeks through December and January, with only Christmas Day and Boxing Day off. The radiotherapy had to be delivered in exactly the same spot every day. Accuracy was critical, so they tattooed my hips with a couple of dots in order to ensure that they hit the exact same area every session.

Once the treatment was completed, we had to leave it for a couple of months and then I would have fresh biopsies to see how much, if at all, the tumour had shrunk. This, in turn, would make the surgery more viable and more likely to have a positive outcome. The months passed quickly, then Sarah and I made the journey to see Mr Briggs for the results.

We entered Mr Brigg's consultation room and sat down to await the news. I was sick to my stomach with nerves.

He looked down at what must have been the results, then shifted his gaze to me and said, 'I don't really know how to tell you this.'

My heart sank.

He continued. 'We have taken the biopsies across your pelvis, from front to back, top to bottom and we cannot detect any live tumour, anywhere.'

Sarah and I were in complete shock; this was the *last* thing we ever expected him to say.

Mr Briggs went on. 'Whatever you have or have not been doing, keep on doing it. We will have you in for another set of biopsies in three months and, all being well, we'll just see you for regular check-ups over the next couple of years.'

The experimental treatment I had gone through was not designed to cure me but to reduce the tumour enough to make surgery a viable option. Although a big sceptic at the time, it would have been stupid of me to completely dismiss the idea that Oliver the faith healer might have had something to do with this result.

I never, ever mentioned the faith healer to Mr Briggs. As far as I was concerned, clinicians who had dedicated twenty-plus years to learning the science of medicine and becoming an expert in their field did not deserve to then be told 'a man who had a car accident when he was a child and got visited by "spirits" placed his hands on me and made me better.'

For probably the first time in my fairly traumatic life, a

medical professional told me that I did not have any more cancer in my body. This was in April 1996.

You can only imagine the euphoria Sarah and I felt. At the lowest point of the past few months, we had previously discussed whether, if I came through this, we would take our relationship to the next stage.

Meeting John Moncur at Upton Park...midfield maestro!

I had met Harry after he wrote to me when I was in Barts. This was a reunion a few years later

7

THE ROCKET:
COME FLY WITH ME!

The next phase of my life had begun. Sarah and I had just got married, and we moved out of the Young Ones' house and rented a small flat together. It wasn't long before we decided to buy our first house, in Aylesbury, Buckinghamshire.

As we were to reside in Aylesbury, we needed to register with a local GP. We did all the usual form-filling requirements needed to get accepted, including providing a urine sample. When the results returned, one of the practice nurses asked me if I was diabetic. She must have seen my eyes roll as I said, 'I hope not, after all the other stuff I have been through!'

The nurse said, 'Don't worry about it for now, but there are signs of sugar in your urine. Go off on holiday and we can pick it up on your return.'

After the holiday, the surgery started to investigate the sugar in my urine. Blood tests and other investigations highlighted the fact that my kidney function was impaired;

apparently, it was functioning at around 65 %. It was suggested that I should see a specialist to establish whether an ongoing management programme would be required.

I was referred to the John Ratcliffe Hospital, which is a famous hospital in Oxford not too far away from us in Aylesbury. I went to see the doctor there; we sat down, talked about the situation and I had more blood tests and scans. On acquiring the results of the tests, we sat down to review the feedback. I was told my kidneys were about 50 % the size they should be, but I was given no explanation as to why that would be. Could I have been born with this deformity? I didn't know – I hadn't experienced any adverse effects from it thus far.

The decision was made that they would repeat the kidney function blood tests. They were particularly looking for the enzyme creatinine, as this gives an indication of your kidney performance. A normal kidney function has a creatinine level of around sixty; mine was around two hundred. If it were to reach a thousand, I'd be in chronic renal failure (CRF) and in need of dialysis.

The tests were repeated over the course of the next year. They showed a continuous increase in creatinine and a subsequent decrease in my kidney function. The doctor plotted a graph of the results, concluding that, if the trend remained the same, by the year 2000 (just four years away) I would be in CRF. Because of this, we talked about the need for dialysis. Haemodialysis is very invasive; it needs to be done three or four times a week and takes around five hours to complete. Basically, your blood is pumped through a machine that cleans it before returning it back into your body. Many people's lives are controlled by the need for regular dialysis.

As part of the requirement for haemodialysis, the doctors informed me that I would have an arteriovenous fistula put in. A fistula is a surgical procedure where they open up your wrist under general anaesthetic and join a vein into an artery. This makes it possible to put the dialysis needle into your wrist on a regular basis, without causing the vein to collapse.

On one of my many visits to the John Ratcliffe, I saw a poster promoting a sponsored abseil, down all ten stories of the hospital building, to raise money for the renal centre and kidney research. After a talk with the organisers and the indemnity forms signed, I was good to go.

The big day of my abseil had arrived. Thanks to my colleagues at work, I had raised around two thousand pounds in sponsorship. There I was, standing on the roof of this ten-story building with quite a breeze blowing. The event was being run by the military, so by all accounts, we were in safe hands.

Harnessed up, I was told to stand on the edge of the building. Keeping my feet where they were I then had to lean back over the precipice. At this point, my whole body was telling me that this was *not* a natural thing to be doing.

As I edged over, my false leg slipped down, as I had no control over it and so gravity took over.

After the initial terror of going over the edge and the realisation I was abseiling on just my right leg, after only half a dozen jumps off the wall, I was on the ground again. I was the only amputee to have taken part, which left me with an enormous sense of achievement.

Allied Dunbar, the company I worked for, was well known for its incredible incentive programme for the Sales team. High achievers were taken off to attend all-expenses-paid exotic locations for 'conferences'. The company ran a league table; the top performers, along with their partners, would be invited to attend such a conference. It was a massive motivation for me and for the sales team as a whole.

As you may recall, I was off from work being treated for cancer for a lot of the earlier part of my employment at Allied Dunbar. However, my boss, Jo Ranger, took on my workload and kept business coming in from my clients during my absence. Thanks to Jo's efforts, by the time I had returned to work, I qualified for the trip to Lisbon, and they insisted that I went.

It was amazing. However, the most memorable such trip was in 1998, to the Ritz Carlton in Cancun, Mexico. It was luxury all the way; we handed our luggage over in the UK, and the next time we saw it was in our room at the Ritz Carlton.

On arrival at the venue, there was a welcome party hosted by the sales director. At the party, everyone was given a 'welcome pack' that included an itinerary of events, enough cash to cover meals when we had free time, and a single raffle ticket (which none of us took any notice of). Once the formal welcome was over, we were told to take out our raffle ticket, as it was for a prize; the winner would get their room upgraded to a suite for the entire week.

I had never won anything before, so I really didn't take a great deal of notice of what was going on. I carried on talking to a mate while we sipped on our cocktails. Something made me look up; the sales director was waving around a raffle ticket and shouting out 'Ticket number 365...?'

He was looking in my direction. I nonchalantly looked down at my ticket and, to my utter amazement, it was number 365. I was about to be upgraded to a suite at the Ritz Carlton, for an entire week. Happy days!

On a few of the organised trips and tours, we regularly passed a water park called Aquaworld, which was just down the road from our hotel. A few of us agreed we should check it out and see if they had any jet skis to rent. A day or two later me, three of the guys and one of the girls, Lorraine, went off to Aquaworld in search of adventure.

We were in luck; they did have jet skis, so me and the guys started to get kitted up, ready for the water. I decided it would not be a good idea for me to go in with my leg on, as it was very heavy, not waterproof and would have been disastrous if I had fallen in with it on – I would easily have sunk to the bottom.

An hour or so later, back on dry land, I put my leg back on and we moved on, fully intending to leave the park and head back to our hotel. On our way out, however, we noticed a thrill ride called the 'Rocket', which was rather like a massive reverse bungee, in that it fired you up rather than you diving down. The cage resembled a large hamster wheel dangling between two towers and attached to what could only be described as giant bungees. The cage was pulled down and secured to the ground, thereby increasing the tension in the bungees. Once its victims were securely strapped in, there was a count down, following which the cage was released, shooting into the Cancun sky.

After my abseil off a ten-story building, I had no fear of this challenge. I asked who was going to join me; while none of the boys were up for it, Lorraine, the only girl in the group, said she'd go on with me. We climbed into the hamster wheel, sat down and were tightly strapped in. While the boys were not too keen to try it, they suddenly found bags of enthusiasm for jeering me and Lorraine on. We felt the cage slowly lock into position and the bungees stretch to full tension. An automated count down began: five, four, three, two, one – and we were launched into the sky at great speed. The cage was spinning almost uncontrollably, doing numerous rolls and bounces, meaning that the g-force was tremendous – my whole body was shaking.

As the spinning slowed and the bouncing subsided, I looked across at Lorraine and asked her if she was alright. We were still at least 50 feet up.

'Yes,' she said. 'How about you?'

I replied in the affirmative, then looked down at my lap and nearly had a heart attack there and then: my false leg had gone! It was no longer connected to me or my stump, and it was not in the cage – it was nowhere to be seen. Wondering where on earth had it had gone, I was suddenly overwhelmed with a mixture of panic and fear. The sea was a hundred yards in front of us and the main Cancun dual carriageway was just a short distance behind. What if my leg had hit someone on the beach or caused a crash on the dual carriageway? The thought of the potential for tragedy terrified me.

As we were slowly being lowered to the ground, I could see my mates, all rolling around on the floor – legs in the air, in fits of hysterical laughter. As I started to scan the horizon to my left, I could see what looked like a uniformed security officer climbing over the perimeter fence and back into the park. As I looked closer, I could see he was carrying something under his arm that looked just like a false leg. As the cage came to a stop, the operators opened the door and the security officer walked up, took one look at me and wordlessly held the leg out in my direction as if to say 'This must be yours'. I gratefully took it from him and looked it over; unbelievably, everything was intact – even my brand-new white trainer was still in place.

Amazingly, the initial velocity that you experience when you are launched into the sky is so great that my leg was literally sucked off of me and spun high into the Cancun sunshine. Once the boys had calmed down and gained a level of sensibility, they explained to me that, as the cage had reached its maximum height, my leg came flying out of the top, carrying on for another fifty feet into the air like a giant boomerang, before descending and coming to rest in the middle of the road – with a security officer in hot pursuit.

One of the guys pointed out that we didn't have a video camera with us, and that we needed to go back and get one from the hotel, come back and do it again. My answer to that was a resounding 'No way!'.

It was time to leave. We were going to get a taxi from the rank, just outside the park gates. We were in luck: there was one waiting. We jumped in, and I clambered into the front, next to what you would consider a typical Mexican taxi driver to look like, with a droopy moustache and a cigarette hanging out the corner of his mouth. As I settled in, he glanced across and stared at my false leg, which was protruding below my shorts. Suddenly he started screaming and shouting at me, repeatedly pointing to my leg and then up to the sky. It became obvious that he must have been sat in his taxi waiting for a fare when my leg had come hurtling over the fence. By the time I had reassured him my leg was back on to stay this time, he continued us on our journey back to the hotel.

On the last night of every conference trip, the sales director liked to make a speech. This year, his speech featured an incident at a nearby waterpark that was very familiar to us, his captive audience.

That was nowhere near the end of it. On arrival back in the UK, it appeared that everyone at head office seemed to know about 'the Rocket incident'. In fact, a full year later I was holding a talk for one of my biggest clients at a hotel in Oxford. Having a drink at the bar that evening, I was trying to shake off a bit of pain and discomfort after standing up all day. The guy standing next to me asked if I was OK, so I explained to him that I had a false leg and had been stood up all day, so was beginning to feel a bit uncomfortable.

The guy suddenly became very animated and said that he had heard such a funny story about a guy and a false leg at a waterpark in Mexico. Of course, the story was my story. By that point, however, it had become somewhat embellished; in his version, both legs flew off and one killed a Mexican outright. I told him that the story was true, that the person was me and that, if he didn't believe me, my ride-partner Lorraine was sitting just a few yards away from us. 'Go ask her if it's true!' I told him.

A few more weeks later, I had a meeting with one of my customers, who I'd known for some time. We were having a bit of a catch up when he asked me how things were going with my kidneys. I gave him the update about how they were deteriorating, saying that the doctors expected me to end up in renal failure by the year 2000.

'Did you not go and see a faith healer when you had the tumour in your pelvis?' he asked.

'Yes.'

'Have you not been back?'

I said no.

'Then you're an idiot. I've got a shoulder problem I need looking at – what are you doing on Thursday?'

Thursday came and we took the day off work and headed for Westcliffe. I was still a cynic, even after my miraculous pelvis recovery. We arrived at Oliver's house; sadly, his mother had died, so he was on his own. It was a lovely sunny day, so he took us out into his back garden.

Tim asked if he could go first, whereupon Oliver proceeded to do the same 'hands over the body' thing as before, stopping at Tim's shoulder. Oliver talked to both of us about a person's aura and the need to align it so that it could self-heal.

After Tim's session was over, Oliver turned to me. He rubbed his hands before moving them over my body. When he got to my lower back, he stopped.

'It's here isn't it?' he asked.

Just like the first time, he warmed his hands and I felt enormous heat as he worked on my lower back.

Now, I was expected to reach renal failure by the year

2000. By the end of that year, all my tests showed that my decline had plateaued. As I write this book in 2021, I have *still* not reached renal failure. Twenty-three years after my second visit to Oliver, and I'm not even in need of dialysis.

On the question of 'Does faith healing work?', maybe, just maybe, my two visits to Oliver might have reduced my cynicism somewhat.

The following year, I was at the limb-fitting centre for a few adjustments to my leg. I started up a conversation with a guy sitting next to me. He asked me what sort of exercise I did, and I had to confess that I did very little.

'You can ride a bike, can't you?' he said.

I hadn't ridden a bike since I was fifteen, I hadn't even tried – the thought had never entered my mind. As a young boy and even as a young teenager, riding a bike was something that we loved to do and would cycle miles to see friends in neighbouring villages.

Not that I'm impulsive, but after Roy had brought my leg back and fitted it, I left the centre and went straight to the nearest Halfords. I talked to the sales guy and bought a bike for £100. We discussed how I would keep my false foot on the pedal. He suggested that I use toe loops; I would put my false foot in the loop and do it up tight – it should then stay well fixed to the pedal.

I hurried home and got the bike set up with the toe clips on the pedals. I steadied myself against the car, keeping my right foot on the floor and my left (false) foot securely in the toe loop. All I needed now was the courage to push off from my car and start pedalling. With a nervous heave, I launched myself forward and started pedalling with my right foot, the left one following.

It all came flooding back. The old saying was true; you never forget how to ride a bike. Childhood memories swirled as the wind hit my face; it was an amazing feeling. I cycled out of the close, out of the estate and all the way across town to a mate's house.

Exhausted, I rang his doorbell. He had the shock of his life when he saw me sat on his doorstep, drenched in sweat from riding a bike.

That short journey was to be the start of some incredible adventures, as I pedalled my bike across places, I never thought I would ever see.

The infamous Rocket Ride, just like the one in Cancun

The cage from which my leg was propelled into the sky!

8

WELCOME BACK:
ON YER BIKE, SON

After the initial diagnosis of my kidney condition, it was decided that it could just be regularly monitored. In the meantime, my life resorted back to some sort of normality, with an occasional visit to the renal unit and a once-a-year visit to the cancer hospital. This was a fairly decent period, thankfully devoid of any major illnesses or the need for frequent visits to the various hospitals from my past.

I was still working for Zurich, now in a role that took me up and down the country presenting to financial advisers on the subject of inheritance tax planning. Things went very well in that role; my confidence was now at an all-time high and I found that the bigger the audience I had to present to, the more of a buzz I got from doing it. Year after year I would qualify for the overseas conventions and, amazingly, got to see wonderful places such as Bali, Singapore, Jamaica, Whistler, Dubai, and New Orleans. I was also regularly enjoying my major passion of going to football with John, who had, by now, introduced me to his cousin Gez. We three had registered with the England Supporters' Club and were travelling all over the world to watch the national side play (in addition to following West Ham home and away every weekend, of course).

The Football Association ran a supporter priority system. This, quite simply, meant that the more games you went to, the more 'caps' you earned. The more caps you earned, the more chance you had of securing tickets when major tournaments came around. Ultimately, that was everyone's goal; we all wanted to see our side play in the Euros and the World Cup.

I remember one year when West Ham had been relegated from the EFL Championship but had got themselves into the playoff final, with a chance to bounce straight back into the Premier League. Unfortunately (which was typical of the Football Association (FA)) this massive game coincided with two England friendlies in the USA. Going to England away games earned you double caps, which would, of course, help improve your priority for tournament games, particularly when tickets were scarce.

After some deliberation, John, Gez and I decided we should go and watch England in the USA. The first game was in Chicago: England v USA at the Soldier Field Stadium. The second game was in New York: England V Columbia at the Giants Stadium. This one was on the same day as our beloved West Ham were playing their most important game of the season. If they won the playoff, they would win a return to the Premier League, dubbed the richest game in football.

Fortunately, the time difference meant that the West Ham game was at nine in the morning, so we found a pub in Greenwich Village that was showing the game. It was absolutely heaving with Hammers fans. What could be better than watching your favourite team in a pub, in Greenwich Village, New York, with two of your best mates, surrounded by fellow Hammers and with an England game still to come later that afternoon? Not only that, but we had also decided to throw in a little culture to our trip; we had tickets to see *Phantom of the Opera* on Broadway in the evening. It was a truly fun-packed day.

To be honest, trying to cram all that into one day, in 30 °C heat and all on one leg was a challenge. Thankfully, John and Gez were always mindful of how difficult it was for me to keep up, so we would rely on taxis wherever possible to limit the amount of walking we did. In fact, one of the highlights of that day was the crazy and frantic 8.5-mile taxicab journey from Giants Stadium to try and make the start of the Phantom show on Broadway with just 20 minutes in hand. To this day, I don't know how, but we actually made it.

Although I was having a great deal of fun following football everywhere with my mates, my relationship with

Sarah was starting to change. We still got on OK, but I was spending more time either at work or with my mates and she was doing the same with hers. Over the next few years, we started to drift apart; eventually, amicably, we agreed that we should get a divorce and go our separate ways. Looking back, I think that I was slightly selfishly catching up on the youth I never really had the time to enjoy. As much as I enjoyed being married, I hadn't really had a chance to do all of those things that most people do *before* they get married. Something had to give.

When you make such a monumental decision, you tend to change other things too. Where you live and your job are two great examples, so off I went. Around this period, I had been approached by a company who had its head office in the Isle of Man. I met with the sales director, did the interviews and, shortly after, got the nod. The only thing I knew about the Isle of Man was that, back in the seventies, my parents had taken us there for a holiday. I recalled crossing the Irish Sea on a ferry from Liverpool and I remembered seeing the famous Laxey Wheel, which is synonymous with the Isle of Man.

My new company was Canada Life International. Shortly after I started at Canada Life, Sarah and I agreed to sell the house and split the equity between us to give us both a start on our next adventure. I moved into temporary accommodation in the interim, renting a nice house in Guildford from my friend, Richard.

After about two months of joining Canada Life, the sales team and I were invited to the company's Christmas party, which was to be held on the Isle of Man. This time, there were no ferries, just a short plane ride from Birmingham to Ronaldsway; in about an hour, we were there. The Christmas party allowed me to meet all of the head office staff in a fun and relaxed atmosphere.

I was chatting to my boss when he pointed across the room and said, 'See that lady over there? Her name is Lynn, and it would be well worth introducing yourself to her, as she's the manager of the new business processing team.'

Lynn and I hit it off immediately. We had a few laughs together that evening; I made sure that she knew I would be relying heavily on her support in order for me to do well at the company, and she made it very clear to me that no such favours would be forthcoming without the accompaniment of suitable bribes. From that point on, we both knew that we had a similar sense of humour.

The evening came to an end, I said my farewells until my next visit, and we looked forward to working together in the new year.

After a few months of working together and speaking to each other on the phone almost every day, we eventually started a relationship outside of work. This was to be another long-distance arrangement; I would fly over to the Isle of Man for the occasional visit and Lynn would fly over to stay for the odd night here and there with me.

Lynn being head of the new business department, and the complete professional that she was, had nothing to do with me being acknowledged as the number-one business development manager at Canada Life later that year, or the trophy I received at a prestigious black-tie dinner in London.

As the relationship developed, it was eventually agreed that Lynn, who was a mother of two children (James aged ten and Nicole aged five), would move with them over to the UK to live with me.

I made the pilgrimage in my car to pick up Lynn, Nicole, James, their pet rottweiler Elka and as much personal stuff as we could fit into both of our cars. By this time, I had bought a house in West Sussex, where the four of us and Elka the Rottie would set up home.

Lynn, having now left the company's head office on the Isle of Man, needed to find a new job local to where we lived. She eventually settled in with a local company, operating their helpdesk. We had placed both James and Nicole into their respective schools, at which point I was approached by Zurich to see if I would consider returning. I was delighted to be invited to go back; my new role would involve working with a team based in Reigate, Surrey.

One evening, a group of us from the office were out having a meal. One member of the team was a lady called Midge; she ran one of the company's charities, called 'Cares 4 Kids'. Over dinner, Midge asked me if it was true that, although I had a false leg, I could still ride a bike?

'Yes, I can,' I replied. 'A little, at least.'

Midge then suggested that I would be a great fundraising attraction for the charity's up-and-coming bike-riding challenge. I said I would be up for that and immediately, with great enthusiasm, asked what her next project was.

Her response was not quite what I expected.

'A 450 km ride in Kerala, South India?' My jaw hit the table. 'You're joking!'

All I had managed so far was a few miles out and around the town where I lived. How on earth was I going to manage this monumental task? I had lost my left leg above the knee and half of my left lung, this was certainly going to be tough but somehow, I was driven to try and prove that regardless of my physical limitations, I was going to succeed at this challenge!

Anyway, not wanting to shy away from a challenge, I agreed to give it a shot. You pay a fee to go and then you are given a fundraising target. We went on a mission to raise the money any way that we could; after all, it was 'for the kids'. We held quiz nights, raffles, curry nights (sticking with the theme, you see) and took advantage of all the obvious fundraising avenues you could think of. I carried a sponsorship form with me everywhere that I went and tried to secure sponsorship from all my clients, constantly playing on the 'one leg' aspect. I also started to put in the miles in an attempt to get my endurance and fitness up, though there is no way to replicate the conditions of South India when you live near South Croydon.

It wasn't long before the trip was upon us, and the team of (mostly) athletic modern cyclists gathered at Heathrow to prepare for our 10-hour flight to India via Dubai.

The Kerala ride would take place over five days. The first day would be relatively flat, so as to ease us into the change of climate; however, days two, three and four would have some significant climbs as we reached as high as 5,000 feet above sea level. Day five would start with a lovely long downhill ride, followed by a long stint along the coast to finish the 450 km journey.

Now, I may very well have been engaging in a charitable project, but it did still manage to cause a little bit of friction at home. Even though I had *never* shown any interest in travelling to India, it turned out that one of the things on Lynn's bucket list was to go there and see the elephants close up. Here I was, in India and, the day before the bike ride was due to start for real, we were scheduled to visit an elephant rescue sanctuary, where I ended up bathing an Indian elephant in the river with a coconut shell. I knew this was something that Lynn would have loved to have done. As you could imagine, I tried to play it down as much as I could, but it really was an amazing experience.

The first day of riding came, with about thirty people at the starting point. There was an incredible buzz in the atmosphere as everyone prepared to set off on this herculean adventure. Some of them had done as many as ten of these challenges and so were incredibly fit. It would be those fit guys who would come alongside me when I was struggling, placing their hands on my back just to give me a little push when the going started to get tough. You can't imagine how hard it is for someone to do that and cycle up a hill themselves, with only one hand on their own handlebars. Incredible.

Day three was epic; the climb was so intense that I just couldn't make my way up the steep inclines. I had to take full advantage of our support bus to help me get to the top of some of the highest peaks.

The overnight accommodation between riding days was about as basic as you could possibly imagine. In one 'hotel' there wasn't even enough running water to have a proper shower at the end of a long sweaty ride. The diet all week was vegetable curry – not my favourite dish!

Day five was an exhilarating downhill experience, as we descended the mountain that we had just spent the past three days climbing. There then followed a long stretch along the coast to the finish. The euphoria that comes from completing such a challenge is immense and really very difficult to put into words. There was a lot of emotion and quite a few tears as everybody united in the relief and gratification of the achievement that they had all experienced. The friendships you make on such a journey are for life. Personally, my satisfaction and sense of achievement were off the scale.

Challenges like these make you realise just what and who is important in your life. I was crying when I called Lynn at the end, full of emotion and with an undying urge to share, with the woman I loved, my immense sense of pride and fulfilment.

After a couple of days recuperating, we flew straight back to Heathrow, where Lynn was waiting to greet me. On seeing Lynn, I immediately realised just how important she was to me, and so I proposed at the airport.

She said yes.

My new family, Lynn, James and Nicole

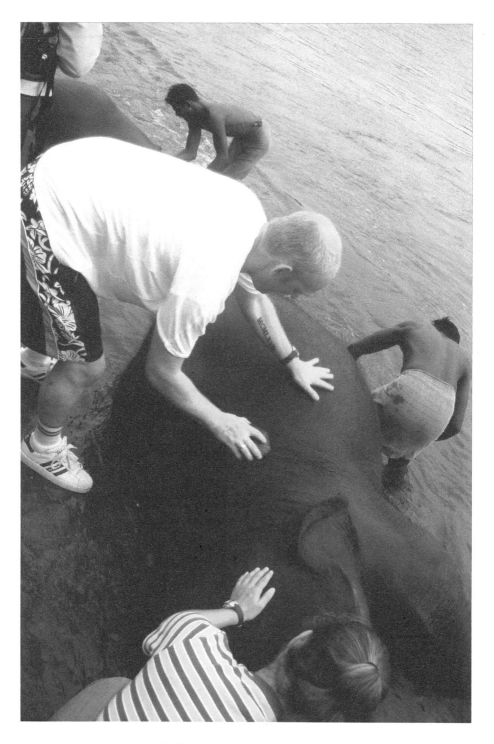

Bathing the baby elephant whilst in India

At the emotional end of the India bike ride with my "team", who helped through day five

9

BACK IN THE USSR: IT'S FOR YOU!

After proposing to Lynn on my emotional return to Heathrow, it was now time to plan our wedding. We were now living as a family; so, before we started planning, we sat and reflected on some of the amazing memories we had already created for our family. We recalled the time that we decided to surprise James and Nicole with an adventure we hoped they would remember for the rest of their lives: a secret trip to Lapland to visit Father Christmas. Nicole was still young enough to believe he was real, James less so by then. Anyone who has visited Lapland will know that these trips are quite expensive, given that you are only in Lapland for a few days. However, the excitement the trip generated was well worth the investment.

Lynn and I had decided to buy James a snowboard for Christmas and wondered how we could get it to Lapland for 'Santa' to have left it for him. After a quick conversation with the company organising the trip, we seemed to have found the solution: one of the reps, who frequently flew over to the resort, would take it before our arrival.

Lynn and I had a plan for the morning of our departure. We needed to get up around four o'clock, so Lynn would go in and wake Nicole and show her the Lapland brochure. She'd reveal that in fact we were going there, not to London (which is what we had told her the night before, when we wanted her to go to sleep early). I would video it all, thereby recording the excitement of her realisation that she was going to see Santa, at his home, in Lapland. We crept into her room, gently woke her, and started to put our plan in place.

Her reaction? She burst into tears! It turned out she really did want to go to London!?

We went to the airport, where there were lots of other excited kids waiting to board the plane to Lapland. The flight went quite quickly, as I think we all slept! As the plane started to descend into Lapland, we could see that it was covered in snow. The excitement started to build.

On arrival, we were greeted by groups of elves who played around the luggage carousel, interacting with the children brilliantly. We were then directed to a building where we picked up all our thermal gear. Although we had brought our own ski clothing, temperatures in Lapland could go as low as -20 °C, so those special thermals were necessary, in order to help keep you warm.

We arrived at our hotel; it was covered in snow, looking

incredibly Christmassy. Upon reaching at our room, we opened the door to see a long present lying on one of the beds. James knew straight away what it was (and who it was from!). We told him he should open it. Nicole was very disappointed that there were no presents waiting for her; we managed to cheer her up by saying that Santa was told she was going to London, so had planned to drop her presents off at our house, and that we were sure they would be there under the tree by the time we got home.

You have to give it to the organisers; they had the perfect format. On the last day, visitors would board a sledge, which was pulled by a snowmobile. The driver would ask the parent if they had 'the ticket' for the ride. This ticket was actually a letter that the child had written to Santa some weeks earlier, which you never really posted to the North Pole but instead took with you on the day.

Off we went through the snow and the tree-lined tracks, until a log cabin came into sight, smoke billowing out from its chimney. As we got closer, the snowmobile slowed down and two elves ran out and played with Nicole and James in the snow. Meanwhile, the driver took the ticket into the cabin and gave it to Santa.

After playing in the snow for a little while, Nicole and James were ushered into the cabin, where Santa was sat next to a roaring log fire.

'You must be Nicole,' Santa said, in a deep but friendly voice.

Nicole was beside herself. She was so excited; her face was a picture. I will never forget that moment. The whole trip was an amazing experience, all of which we recorded on video, but which I'm sure will last in all of our memories for many years to come.

On my return to work in the new year, Midge (the lady who ran the company charity) approached me to ask if I would do another charity bike ride. This time, it was in Cuba – another destination Lynn had always wanted to visit.

It wasn't long before that trip was upon us, by which point the funds had been raised and miles put into the legs. We all met up again at the airport; as it turned out, many of the Kerala team were also on the Cuba trip.

This ride stretched from the Bay of Pigs to Havana, some 350 km. It passed through some amazing countryside and was flatter than the Indian trip, but much hotter. The sights of Cuba were awesome, the architecture and all the old cars were certainly some of the highlights along the trek.

During the ride, I was looked after by Cuba's equivalent to Lance Armstrong (but without the drugs), who helped me out with a hand on my back whenever I needed it. I have a photo that someone had taken behind us, with him alongside me and his hand on my back helping me up a hill. I thought it was very symbolic. There have been people there to help me every step of the way, from my mate driving out to fetch me cheeseburgers twice in a row, to Lynn's incredible support and care. Cycling up that hill, I remembered every other challenge I'd faced, and the hands-on my back that have supported me.

As was the case in India, the end of the ride was extremely emotional and exhilarating for all of us, both individually and as a team. Again, on arrival home, I had to play down how fantastic the adventure had been, so as not to rub it in for Lynn. I have, of course, promised to take her there one day, when I'm sure we will get to enjoy Cuba together.

Travel with a purpose was very much part of my life. I travelled to take part in the charity rides, which raised money for worthwhile causes. I also travelled with John and Gez, supporting the England football team. The next trip in the England football calendar was for a game in Moscow. We decided to make our own travel arrangements, so we didn't stay in the designated England fan hotel in the centre of Moscow. Instead, we chose a boutique hotel on the outskirts of the city centre, which had its own sort of hotel taxi that would ferry you to wherever you wanted to go. It was worth the extra cost to stay somewhere all the other England fans were not!

There had been a postal strike in the UK before our departure, so the FA advised all travelling fans to pick up their tickets at a certain location near the grounds. We asked the hotel driver to take us so that we could get there early to pick up the tickets and stay away from any potential trouble, as there were rumours that Moscow thugs were out to cause havoc with the England fans.

We then watched the game, before deciding to leave a few minutes early. Having a false leg helps when you are negotiating with Russian security guards to leave the stadium five minutes early, so you can meet your driver and get away before any trouble might start.

It was a great cultural trip, and we saw many of Moscow's most famous landmarks. Fortunately, at no point did we see any trouble. However, when we arrived back at the airport to go home, the departure lounge resembled a scene from *Casualty*, with black eyes and bandages everywhere. It turned out that the Russian hooligans had stormed the large hotel where all the England fans were staying and there was no escape for many who suffered at their hands.

Once back at home, I started to plan a business presentation I was to deliver to a group of clients at Aston Villa's grounds, Villa Park. I decided I wouldn't drive and had to work out the best way to get there using trains and a taxi.

I began my presentation and, halfway through it, I started to feel very dizzy and sweaty. Somehow, I got through the presentation, but declined the offer of lunch. I was a long way from home and all I wanted to do was get back there.

When I eventually got home, I felt dreadful, so put myself straight to bed.

I was to stay in bed for the next four days; I was hallucinating, sweating, and couldn't eat or drink anything. Lynn was so concerned she phoned 111 and they told her to keep a close eye on me and, if it got worse, to phone back. By the weekend, I had deteriorated to such an extent that Lynn phoned again. Their response this time was to arrange for a doctor to visit the house.

When the doctor arrived, he asked me a few questions before asking if he could use the house phone, using it to call for an ambulance, which arrived within 10 minutes and whisked me off to East Surrey hospital. After a series of tests, I was told that I had viral pneumonia.

I didn't recall feeling quite so ill for a very long while, and I spent a week in hospital before being allowed to go home. On the day of my return home, it was Bonfire Night, but I just didn't have the strength to go to the local firework display as we'd planned.

As often happens when you're unwell, you suddenly become very aware of your condition's appearance in the news; I learned that West Ham legend Frank Lampard's mum and TV star Jeremy Beadle had both recently died from pneumonia. As it turned out, lots of people die from pneumonia – I'd had another close shave!

A couple of weeks later, I was in London, attending a meeting. I was coming back in a cab around seven in the evening when my phone rang, I didn't recognise the number, but answered it anyway. It was Mr Briggs' secretary.

Now, everyone knows it's not going to be good news when a consultant's secretary calls you at seven o'clock in the evening on a Friday.

'Sorry to call you so late, but Mr Briggs has asked to see you at the Royal National Orthopaedic Hospital in Stanmore, first thing Monday,' she said. 'I'm afraid I don't know any more than that.'

My heart sank. I went into freefall; the panic button had been well and truly pressed. What on earth could be wrong that needed a call on a Friday evening? I didn't get much sleep over that weekend, as we tried to come to terms with the situation and the potential outcome.

Monday morning arrived, and we made the trip to Stanmore for 9am. As we sat in the waiting room, my phone rang again. It was Mr Briggs himself, saying he would be with us in twenty minutes but, just to put my mind at rest, there was nothing for us to worry about.

The outcome was that someone at East Surrey hospital, where I was treated for pneumonia, had spotted something unusual on one of my chest x-rays that they thought looked a little sinister; a small 'nodule' on one of my lungs. They looked up my records and saw that I was under Mr Briggs' observations for cancer, so reported it directly to him, without contacting me.

My relationship with Mr Briggs was such that he wanted to get me in as soon as possible, so that he could do some tests. He wanted to prove what he suspected all along: that what they had seen in East Surrey hospital was simply scar tissue from my previous lung surgery. The tests, of course, corroborated this theory.

The relief was overwhelming.

Good news led to even better news, as Lynn and I could now finish organising our wedding. Lynn suggested that we needed to choose a date that meant I couldn't forget our wedding anniversary. Lynn's birthday was the 25th, while mine was the 13th. Right in the middle of our birthdays (nine days from each) was the 4th so that was the date we decided to get married on.

We had both been married previously, so we decided to have a small ceremony at a local hotel, with immediate family as our guests and with 'West Ham John' as my best man. The following night, we had an amazing party at our house, with all our friends there to celebrate with us. It was a night when many bubbles were drunk – there certainly were a few very sore heads in the morning.

One day at work, a colleague came up to me and said, 'I've got a friend called Kiera who's also an amputee. You should meet her.'

My colleague went on to tell me that Kiera was responsible for a charity called LimbPower, which introduces amputees back into sport. Every year, LimbPower would hold a weekend event at Stoke Mandeville, where people with all forms of limb impairment could go and try out a variety of sports. I got in touch with Kiera, and soon got invited to the next Stoke Mandeville sports weekend.

What an amazing weekend that was. To see so many amputees trying new sports was inspirational; in fact, I know that some of those I met went on to represent GB at future Paralympics. Kiera asked me if I would help with the next fundraising event, which turned out to be a cycle ride from London to Paris, to be completed in just three days. I hadn't been on the bike for a little while since Cuba, but I thought, 'I've done it before – I can do it again'.

With that, the training began. The ride was to start from Beckenham in Kent; we would make our way to Dover on the Friday, catch the ferry to Calais, cycle all day Saturday and reach Paris on Sunday afternoon.

There were several amputees undertaking the ride. For my part, I enlisted some of my fitter clients to take part so they could help me out on the tough sections (the hills!). The South Downs presented a serious challenge on the first day and, on the second day, I suffered significant chafing of my stump and had to tape myself up to get through.

We eventually reached Paris, with the finish line being under the Eiffel Tower. Again, reaching our destination, in defiance of all the challenges these rides throw up, is euphoric. This one really did take it out of me though and was likely to be my last.

It was only when I tried to remove my leg in order to get in the shower at the hotel that I realised the damage I had done to myself. My abductor tendon was so swollen (about the size of a golf ball) that I could not get my leg back on and had to leave it off completely for the few days that we had to recuperate in Paris.

I absolutely did feel a great sense of achievement to cycle so far in just three days, and we had raised a great deal of money for LimbPower, but this was definitely to be my last 'big ride'. It was time to hang up my cycling shorts.

After the finish with the whole team in Havana, Cuba - another memorable ride

Gez, John and I outside the Kremlin during our trip to Moscow, Russia

With my wonderful wife, Lynn, on our wedding day

The finish of my last bike ride beneath the Eiffel Tower in Paris

10

BEST JOB OF MY LIFE:
WE'RE ON THE HOME STRAIGHT

Thanks to Mr Briggs, our panic over my most recent health scare was short-lived. I believe this was exactly what Mr Briggs was trying to achieve: to get the issue checked and put to rest as quickly as possible.

The only medical interventions I had now were quarterly visits to the renal team, who needed to monitor my kidney function as, while its deterioration had levelled off, it was still only operating at around 15% of normal kidney function.

Everything was good. Lynn and I were enjoying married life, we were going on regular holidays with the kids and I was enjoying my career. I was still working for Zurich (although I did get head-hunted by another company, I worked for that company for a year, got made redundant and returned back to Zurich for the third time).

During this third period at Zurich, it too went through a reorganisation and made people redundant. Although I had worked for Zurich for fifteen years in total, I had only been with the company for less than a year this time, so the old adage of 'last in first out' applied and I found myself out of a job.

However, Lady Luck was not far away; I met up with a friend who had been my boss at Zurich some years earlier, before he had departed for a new role elsewhere. He explained that a division of the company where he now worked was looking for someone, and that he would introduce me to them.

A short time later, I was invited to a meeting with the managing director and the CEO of a company called Dragonfly. It was a very relaxed meeting, as I had been proposed by someone they respected, who I had worked for in the past. They explained that their core business was short-term property finance such as bridging and buy-to-let mortgages, something I knew very little about. I thought bridges were used to cross rivers and the closest I had come to mortgages lately was having one.

Like many companies, especially customer-facing ones, part of the interview process can include a role play to see how you handle yourself in a sales/negotiation scenario. The interviewers asked me if I would be willing to undertake a role-playing challenge. They gave me the brief and left the room for a few minutes in order to give me time to understand the fictional situation with which I was presented.

The role play was like the rest of the interview: very relaxed. However, as it was an interview for a finance position, obviously the situation we were playing out required a financial calculation to be made. With the help of a calculator, I did the number crunching and, after much clicking on the calculator, I came up with an answer.

The guys looked at each other and burst out laughing.

'What's so funny?' I asked.

One answered, still chuckling. 'It's because we don't know exactly how you did that, but the answer was exactly right!' I think they could tell that I was manically pressing buttons hoping they were the right ones – and as it turned out, they were!

Over the next couple of weeks, I was introduced to various people within the company as part of the acceptance programme. My friend who had initially recommended me to the company told me, off the record, that they all liked me and felt I was a good fit. However, they then interviewed a lady who had been in their industry for twenty years and who had vast experience in the business sector. Eventually, they decided that they would give the job to her.

Obviously, I was bitterly disappointed; in the meantime, however, dependable Zurich had come back with another job offer. I had no real interest in accepting it initially, for several reasons (one of which being that it involved me declining the offer of some redundancy pay) but eventually I decided I would take it, as I needed to work.

Three months into the job, I took a phone call from Dragonfly, who asked me if I was still interested in joining them. I was not enjoying the role at Zurich at all, and so was keen to explore this new opportunity.

I went through the whole interview process again and, this time, got the job. In the preceding three months, they had had someone leave and so a vacancy had become available. True to their word, they called me back. I met the team at their Old Bailey office; they were a great bunch of guys, so I straight away knew it would be a fun place to work.

On the first day, I arrived wearing a tie, as that was the normal dress code for Zurich. Immediately, one of the guys ribbed me, asking if I was off to a funeral or having another interview. The tie came straight off.

At Dragonfly, my career took off. The short-term property finance sector had exploded, and Dragonfly was a very ambitious company, constantly chasing industry awards and striving to be the best. It felt great to be part of such a dynamic organisation. Over the early months I was able to build some strong relationships with clients and partners, to the point we became friends, attending social gatherings outside of the normal business environment.

With Dragonfly's desire to win awards, I decided, in my third year, that I would challenge for the annual Bridging and Commercial Awards, in the category Business Development Manager (BDM) of the Year. The process was based initially on client votes, leading to a long list of 10 BDMs being drawn up, before the judges (who were all industry peers) reduced this to a shortlist of 5. If you were short-listed, you'd have to obtain two written testimonies endorsing you; it is these testimonies that go to the judges' panel, from which they choose the eventual winners.

The winner is announced at an awards dinner, which normally has about 500 people on the guest list. The day of the awards dinner arrived, and the industry's finest descended on the venue, which was in Chelsea. The evening followed a typical awards ceremony format, with categories being announced and winners going up on stage to receive their trophy and the adulation of their peers.

The moment came for the announcement of the winner of my category. There were five of us in the frame, all sitting with our various teams. The compere announced the runner up – it wasn't me. Suddenly, the room was booming with the words '... and the winner of the Business Development Manager of the Year Award is ... Justin Cooper!'

What a rush; I couldn't believe it. My table went berserk, they were cheering and patting me on the back. I was filled with a sense of immense achievement and pride. This was the pinnacle of my career, one that I had worked extremely hard to achieve. The whole experience was surreal. Winning this award meant that you were recognised as the best in the industry and were the envy of your peers. Within three years at Dragonfly, I had made it.

Some months later, Dragonfly's CEO, Jonathan Samuels, left and moved on to another project. It was sad to see Jonathan leave, as he was well respected and liked by all.

One morning, a few months later, I arrived early; Matt Smith, our head of credit and my good friend, was also in. He called me into an empty office, dropping a bombshell on me by telling me that he and our managing director Mark Posniak, my boss, were leaving to join Jonathan in his new venture. The announcement was to be made official later that day. I was devastated; these were guys I loved working with and now, suddenly, they would be gone.

The staff were asked to assemble, and the announcement Matt had given me a heads-up about that morning was made official. The atmosphere was grim. As I got back to my desk, I noticed that I had a text message on my personal mobile. It was from Jonathan, our ex-CEO, asking if I would like to meet with him for a coffee. My heart jumped – did this mean what I hoped it meant?

I took a day off and met with Jonathan, who outlined what he was planning with Matt and Mark, saying that they wanted me to be part of the team. I was delighted, because I loved working with these guys and couldn't wait until I would be doing so again.

The new company was called Octane Capital; it was launched on 1st May 2017. As of August 2021, we have lent more than £1bn, and we are still growing. It is simply the greatest job I've ever had, and I want to keep doing it for as long as my health will allow.

Strangely, I don't think that any of this would have ever happened if I had never developed cancer at such an early age. As a teenager I had my sights on becoming a mechanic but now my life was moving in circles I could never had imagined. My ambition was renewed, and my motivation was exploding. Is there such a thing as fate?

The regular visits to the renal unit showed that my kidney function was still at around 15%. At this level, the clinicians advise that you should be placed on the kidney transplant list, even though you don't need dialysis at this point, as dialysis is needed at about 10% function.

Such low kidney function does have an effect on your day-to-day life. Some days I might feel exhausted and sick, with no appetite, while other days I feel fine.

Kidney transplants are normally made from deceased donors, but now it is becoming more common for relatives and friends to donate a kidney to a loved one, as it's been scientifically proven that we can survive and function normally with one healthy kidney.

One day, when Lynn and I were talking, she announced that she wanted to see if she was a match. If she was, she said she would like to donate one of her kidneys to me. Upon hearing this, I felt incredibly emotional, completely taken aback in shock. Here, the woman I loved was prepared to go through incredible mental and physical trauma to give me a better and longer quality of life. I could not comprehend how she had come to terms with the gravity of such an incredible decision. Part of me felt protective of her and didn't want her to put herself at risk on my behalf, while another part of me couldn't really find the words to tell her how thankful I was.

After the emotional decision had been made, Lynn embarked on the tests to see if she was a match. The results offered both good and bad news. Lynn, unfortunately, wasn't a direct match for me, but we were informed of a kidney-sharing programme, which is a fantastic concept where those who had hoped to donate a kidney to a specific recipient but are not a match can donate to an anonymous recipient, thus making their intended recipient eligible to receive a kidney from someone who is a match for them. The protocols for the kidney-sharing scheme are quite intense. The donor has to go through a series of tests and interviews to establish their physical and mental health; the doctors have to establish the reasons why they are offering their kidney, to ensure that they are not doing it under duress or for money.

Throughout the acceptance process, we were told that physical fitness would play a major part in the success of any such surgery. So, both Lynn and I started going to the gym in order to increase our fitness. We were later told that we would be able to join the program in around October 2020. However, the whole process was brought to a sudden halt when the COVID-19 pandemic hit. The transplant lists were suspended, and the gym was suddenly replaced by the lounge and a laptop screen.

When the lockdown eventually eased, we started to go

back to the office. I was upstairs getting ready for work one morning when I realised that I had to stop getting dressed, as I was completely out of breath. I literally had to sit down on the bed to recover. When I eventually got downstairs, I explained the situation to Lynn and phoned Matt to let him know that I wouldn't be coming into the office as planned, explaining that I was frighteningly out of breath. Matt said that he had noticed how out of breath I was the previous week.

I contacted the renal unit; I think they thought I might have COVID, so suggested that someone should see me as soon as possible. After ringing the doctors who couldn't see me quickly enough, we then tried 111 who said someone would call back. After an hour or so I eventually rang the hospital, who said I had better come down.

Lynn drove me to the nearest A&E, and they took me straight through to the majors' department. There, they took a host of tests and a scan of my chest. Eventually, I got to see a consultant, who said that all the evidence pointed to me having a blood clot on my lung(s) and that I would need to be admitted to the hospital immediately.

I was put onto a ward that Monday night. My breathing was very poor, so I was put on oxygen and given blood-thinning drugs. On the Wednesday, I had a scan using some form of nuclear gas, which I believe is used to try and show any potential clotting on the lungs

The result of the scan showed that I had multiple blood

clots on both lungs, which was clearly why I was struggling to breathe. It was a few more days later, when my blood was eventually thin enough, that it was safe to let me go home. I had been in hospital for eight days. This latest episode meant I would be on the blood-thinning drug warfarin for the rest of my life.

Just like any good TV soap, when one episode closes another one starts, bringing new drama. My next episode started in April 2021, and so did the drama. I was about to take a trip to the dentist when I decided to take a trip to the bathroom first, immediately noticing that my urine was the colour of Ribena. This was a little unnerving, and a bit scary to say the least; however, it only lasted a day and, for the next couple of weeks, everything returned to normal.

About two weeks later, the same thing happened again. I phoned the renal unit, who said that I had haematuria, which is when you have blood in your urine. It doesn't take much blood to make it look bad but, nonetheless, it shouldn't be happening.

I made contact with a GP, who said this needed investigating and arranged for me to have an endoscopy and a CT scan at the local hospital. The result was that they found a 1 cm tumour on the wall of my bladder. This was devastating news to me. By then, I had been clear of cancer for some twenty-five years.

I got home and explained the situation to Lynn, finding

myself feeling very calm. Maybe with everything I had faced over the years, I just saw it as another challenge, or maybe it was because the clinicians said they had found it early and they say when it's found early you have a better chance. Personally speaking, I took the approach that I tell everyone else to take; I won't worry until someone tells me I have something to worry about.

I had private medical insurance through work, so I decided to explore this avenue. I phoned the insurance company, who gave me the names of three of their consultants, two of whom were on the top of a letter I had received from the NHS.

I chose Mr Swinn, as he was at the top of the letter, and went to see him. As I pulled into the car park of the private clinic, my mobile rang; it was the NHS secretary, informing me that they could get me in for the surgery a week on Friday. Knowing I was going in to see Mr Swinn in just a moment, I said I would phone her back in an hour.

Mr Swinn had an air of surety about him; he made me feel that he was in complete control and knew exactly how to handle the situation. He said he didn't think that this current tumour had anything to do with my past, it was just bad luck.

I thought to myself, 'How much bad luck can one guy have?'

Mr Swinn, in his very calm and matter-of-fact manner, said, 'I believe we have caught it very early, and I suspect that it will be what we call non-muscle-invasive bladder cancer.'

He went on to explain that the tumour could be removed with a very simple surgical procedure, and that it might need to be followed up by a six-week course of chemotherapy. After a short discussion, it was agreed I should stay with the NHS, as it was likely that he would end up doing the surgery anyway.

Unfortunately, Lynn had to wait in the car during the appointment, as she wasn't allowed in with me due to COVID restrictions. When I returned, we immediately phoned the NHS secretary back; she informed us that she was in fact Mr Swinn's secretary and that it would indeed be him carrying out the surgery.

We spent the few days prior to the operation with my best mate Darren and his wife Jane down in Portsmouth, having fun and keeping our thoughts away from what was to come at the end of the week. Darren was the mate who had cycled with me to the girls' house all those years ago, when my Mum had got the call to go to the hospital. He'd been with me from back when it all started. It was great to know that I had a mate that was there at the very beginning and still here now, all these years later.

It was Friday 18th June, and I was getting ready for my surgery. It was also the date when England played Scotland in the 2020 (2021) Euros.

As I went through the process of getting prepared for the

general anaesthetic, memories of the same journey all those years ago came flooding back. If you have to have general anaesthetic, to me there is an upside, in that as soon as you regain consciousness, you know the whole thing is over and the recovery has begun.

As I was wheeled into the anaesthesia room, I noticed the time was 11.45am; when I woke up in the recovery room, it was only 12.30pm, so the whole procedure had taken just under forty-five minutes. The doctor came and saw me on the ward and reassured me that everything had gone well and that, as soon as I could produce 250 ml of urine, I could go home. After downing as many jugs of water as I could, followed by some very painful peeing, I reached the required amount and got the green light to go home. Lynn came to collect me, and I was home in time to watch a boring 0–0 draw with Scotland.

A couple of weeks later, the results of the bladder biopsy were in. The result was that the tumour definitely was non-invasive; it was not deep-rooted into the wall of my bladder, merely attached to the surface. There were some moderate low-grade cells, but also some moderate- to high-grade cells, which meant that there was a small risk that it could come back. Therefore, I was to undertake a six-week course of chemotherapy treatment, designed to kill off any lingering cells and reduce the chances of another tumour coming back.

The hospital sent me a very informative booklet on non-muscle-invasive bladder cancer. The new chemotherapy for this particular type of cancer is directed straight into the bladder, so it never enters your bloodstream. Because of this, I have had none of the usual sickness side-effects; it has all been very straightforward and painless. After a chemo session, all I must do is go straight home and pee it away after an hour or so. I have to say that it was a great relief to me to find that this treatment was so non-invasive because previous chemotherapy has generally been so debilitating. I was a little sceptical after reading the booklet, but the reality of the situation was actually far better than they warned.

At the time of writing, I'm still undergoing the six weeks of chemotherapy. After the treatment has ended, I will have to go for another endoscopy, to check to see if any of the tumour has returned.

What originally concerned me, though, was what effect this cancer episode would have on my chances of having a kidney transplant. According to information I had received previously, I believed I would have to have been clear from cancer for at least ten years before I could be eligible for a transplant. Prior to the current situation, I had been clear for 25 years.

I contacted the renal unit to give them an update on what had been going on. They gave me some encouraging news: the rules have changed over the years and so, providing your cancer and subsequent treatment were non-invasive, then the wait could be down to as little as two years.

In two years, I will have been on the transplant waiting list for seven years, meaning I would become what is known as a 'long lister'. The good news is that long listers tend to get the call for a kidney match within just a few weeks. So, in two years' time, I could get the call fairly rapidly, which would mean that Lynn will not have to go through the trauma and pain of donating one of her own kidneys. This doesn't necessarily mean that getting bladder cancer was a good thing but it sort of forced me to have to wait another 2 years and that wait could mean a shorter period for me to be eligible for a deceased donor's kidney.

When I think about this latest incident, I believe it may have happened for a reason, and that that reason will all come to fruition in around two years' time.

Touch wood!

Winning the B&C BDM of the year award was a career highlight for me

A trip to Ireland for Rene's boys to reunite with our old landlord, Kevin

After going to the gym for 18 months, I was able to lift 52.5kg above my head in August 2021. A proud moment for me!

A hug with my best mate who's been there from the start. Friends for life

EPILOGUE

It was upon finding out that I had bladder cancer recently that prompted me to go ahead and write this book, so what was I looking to achieve by doing this?

Despite everything that I have been through medically speaking, I have always felt that I have lived an absolutely amazing life and quite possibly more amazing than if I had never originally contracted bone cancer at 15 years of age.

What I wanted to achieve by writing this book was to firstly try and put a smile on the faces of others who have been or are being affected by this terrible disease, that we now know will touch on average every other person, in one form or another. I have tried to balance the darker days with equally (if not many more) lighter days and that for all the terrible things that cancer has done to me, there have been multiple, life-changing, great things.

Throughout my life I have met many strong and influential people. People who have managed to turn great adversity into triumph. I wanted to share my experiences, in the hope that I might do exactly that for people who will be looking for that glimpse of belief or spark of motivation that is required to overcome what could be, the greatest challenge of their life.

Obviously, when you stop to reflect on all the negative aspects to losing a leg at the age of 17, you can easily understand why someone could spiral into a world of despair and self-pity. Yes of course, I went through periods of asking myself "why me" when I couldn't run or play football anymore, but you only have to look at today's Paralympians and there are young men and women out there who are achieving World Records with all sorts of "disabilities"

Although the amputation was a life-changing operation, as I explained, it *saved* my life more than it ever changed it. Dealing with cancer is a fight many will have lost, but I meet people on an ever-increasing frequency who have beaten this disease and that is testimony to an incredible combination of strength, love, support and ever-improving medical science. I have always believed the mantra that having a positive mental attitude goes a long way to helping someone get through periods of extreme illness. When I was first diagnosed, my naivety was my strength but nowadays people of all ages are much more aware of how dangerous cancer can be and the effect that it can have on someone's life expectancy. If I can spread my story as far as possible it would make me immensely proud if it managed to make a difference to just one person. If I could, I would speak to anyone who needed that lift, on the basis that it is unlikely that I could manage to do that, this book will be the next best thing.

It is not my intention to make any money from selling

this book and I will be passing all profits onto Cancer Research UK. If you are reading this book, it means you have contributed already, so **thank you!** I believe in the power of networking so please tell as many people as you can about this book and the more copies sold, the more will be going to a great cause.

Please take the time to check their website
cancerresearchuk.org

Thank you and good luck
Justin

Lynn arranged for me to meet my all-time favourite actor - Robert De Niro